INDUSTRIAL RELATIONS AND TRADE UNION

According to the New Syllabus Framed by the Various Universities in India for M.B.A., M.P.M. D.B.M., P.G.D.B.M., & F.Y., S.Y., T.Y. B.Com

INDUSTRIAL RELATIONS AND TRADE UNION

By

Dr. Shrinivas V. Joshi

M.Com., M.Phil., LL.M., Ph.D., D.T.L., D.C.L.
D.LL & L.W., G.D.C. & A., M.Com. (Comm)
Karm. A.M. Patil Arts, Commerce
And
Kai. N.K. Patil Science College, Pimpalner
(Dhule) (Maharashtra)

&

Dr. Narendra M. Kadu

M.Sc. (Botany), M.Ed., Ph.D., M.A.
(Sociology, History, Music, Public Administration)
LL.B., D.B.M., Pune
(India)

DISCOVERY PUBLISHING HOUSE PVT. LTD.
NEW DELHI-110 002

Published by:
Tilak Wasan
DISCOVERY PUBLISHING HOUSE PVT. LTD.
4383/4B, Ansari Road, Darya Ganj
New Delhi-110 002 (India)
Phone : +91-11-23279245, 43596064-65
Fax : +91-11-23253475
E-mail : parul.wasan@gmail.com
discoverypublishinghouse@gmail.com
web : www.discoverypublishinggroup.com

***First Edition:* 2013**

ISBN: 978-93-5056-274-1

Industrial Relations and Trade Union

Printed at:
Dynamic Printers
Delhi

Preface

Industrial Relation is one of the most delicate and complex problems of the modern industrial society which is characterized by rapid change industrial unrest and conflicting ideologies in the National and International spheres. It is a dynamic concept which depends upon the patterns of society, economic system and the political set up of a country and changes with the changing economic and social order. It is an arts of living together for the purposes of production, productive efficiency, human well being and industrial progress.

The importance of good Industrial relations and the maintenance of and Industrial pease for raising the tempo of productivity has assumed a high significance in recent times. This has resulted in evolving ways and means of enlarging the area of employer and employee amity and co-operation.

Today one of the major challenges facing the personal and industrial relations staff is the need for sensing the climate of organizations to identify potential or red problems before they became unmanageable.

A critical relationship between the labour and the management is sine-qva-non for industrial peace and productivity. The aim of every employee and employer should be workability stability, peace and harmony.

Trade unionism has to play a vital role in ensuring industrial peace as a democracy to the workers for their judicious demands. Between the management and the workers the trade union acts as a mediator for upholding a smooth relationship between the two and ensuring maximum stability and achievement of efficiency.

Trade union in India widely differ in their approach technological upgradation. The union's approach is influenced by expediency and not by merit. Such unions are least interested to nurse the help of the organization. Their prime interest is to retain or increase membership at organizational cost.

I shall be failing in my duty if I do not specially acknowledge my debt to the members of my family specially to my parents who have suffered untold deprivation to see me established in life. I also express my sincere appreciation to my wife Savita for her valuable assistance in the preparation of this book of proof reading, verifying notes and references.

I thanks my Guru Prin Nandkishor Dayama, Lasalgaon collage (Nashik) (M.S.), Prof. Bapusaheb Deshmukh, Pimpalner, Prof. J.P. Amrutkar and Dr. Shubhash Ahire (Pune).

I am also thankful to the Chief Editor of Discovery Publications and their staff (New Delhi) for having undertaken the responsibility for publishing this work.

All the views expressed in this study and any errors omissions in it. However, are entirely my responsibility. Lastly suggestions are invited for the readers, for improvement of this book for its next edition.

Prof. Dr. Shrinivas V. Joshi
Prof. Dr. Narendra M. Kadu

Contents

Globalization, Liberalization on Trade Union Movement in India—Origin and Historical Development of Trade Union (movement) in India—Social Welfare Period (1875-1918)—Early Trade Union Period (1918-1924)—Left Wing Trade Union Period (1924-1935)—Trade Union's Unity Period (1935-1939)—The Second World War Period (1939-1946)—The Post Independence Period (1947 onwards)—Problems Faced Trade Unions—Small Size and Low Membership—Weak Finances of the Unions—Limited Area and Uneven Growth—Dominance of Outsiders in Union—Multiplicity of Unions and Inter and Intra-union Rivalry—The Problems of Recognition—Union Security—Neglect of Worker's Welfare—Defective Administration—National Commission Labour for Strengthening Trade Unions (1969)—Enlargement of Functions—Leadership—Union Rivalries—Developing Work Culture—Amalgamation—Change in Employer's Attitude—Role of Trade Unions in Increasing Productivity in Industrial Organisations—Role of Trade Unions in Increasing Productivity—Law and Practice Relating to Recognition of Trade Union—Historical Development of Recognition—Law and Practice to Recognition of Trade Unions—Cancellation of Recognition of Union—Rights of Recognized Trade Union under the Code of Discipline—Conclusion—International Trade Unions—International Labour Organization (ILO)—Role/Functions of ILO—Fundamental Principles of ILO—Structure of ILO—Changing Role of Trade Unions in Globalize Economic Environment—Role of Trade Unionism (Trade Union Movement) towards Child Labour—Role of Indian Trade Union Movement for the Women Workers—Role of Trade Union Movement in

CHAPTER 1

Industrial Relations

Introduction

Industrial Relations: Concept

The term 'Industrial Relations' consists on Industry and relations. Thc term industry has been defined under the amendment Act of 1982 of the Industrial Disputes Act, 1947. According to the Section 2 (j), "Industry means any systematic activity carried on by cooperation between an employer and his workmen for the production, supply or distribution of goods and services with a view to satisfy human wants." The industry is an activity where capital and labour cooperate with each other for the purpose of production of the goods and services needed by the society and is the process of making profit.

Under factory system a large number of people having different abilities, skills, aspirations, cultural backgrounds, language etc. come together to work in the organization to satisfy their own needs. So they are interested in higher wages. Whereas management is interested in maximizing profits which calls for keeping wage cost at minimum. Thus, collaboration of men with diverse interests and in altogether different work setting frequently leads to conflicts and tensions as each group tries to maximize its share. Problems of human relationship arising out of the sale of labour for wages and working on the premises of employers under their control form the subject matter of industrial relations. They come into existence and grow out of employment and involve relationship between employers and employees and their organizations.

Labour conditions in modern times develop under State Regulation. The participation of the State in regulating labour-management relations has been steadily increasing. Hence, the concept of industrial denotes not only relations between employers and employees, but also relations of the State with employers, workers and their organizations.

Definition of Industrial Relations

(1) Industrial Relations may be defined as the complex of interrelations among workers, managers and the Government. Prof. Dunlop

(2) Industrial Relations involve attempts to arrive at workable solutions between the conflicting objectives and values, between profit motives and social gains, between discipline and freedom, between authority and industrial democracy, between bargaining and cooperation and interests of the individual, the group and the community. Richard A. Lester

(3) Industrial Relations is that part of management which is concerned with the manpower of the enterprise, whether machine operator, skilled worker or manager. Benthel, Smith and Others

(4) Industrial Relations refer to a dynamic and a developing concept which is not limited to the complex relations between trade unions and management but also refers to the general web of relationships normally obtaining between employers and employees, a web much more complex that the simple concept of labour-capital conflict. Prof. T.N. Kapoor

(5) Industrial Relations in a wide sense denote such matters as freedom of association and the right to organize the application of the principle of the right to organize

and right of collective bargaining of conciliation and arbitration proceeding and the machinery for cooperation between the authorities and the occupational organizations at various levels of the economy.

(6) Industrial Relations in an act, the art of living together for purposes of production. The parties involved in industrial relations *i.e.* the workers and the employers, have a common purpose-production. They willingly bind themselves to work together. It is an art which the two parties learn by acquiring the skills of adjustment. J. Henry Richardson

(7) The field of industrial relations include the study of workers and their trade unions management, employer's associations and the State institutions concerned with the regulation of employment. H.A. Clegg

(8) Industrial Relations deal with the problems which arise in the context of human relationships when the workers submit themselves to being controlled by the employers. Dale Yoder

The industrial relations are an integral aspect of social relations arising out of employer-employee interaction in modern industries, which are regulated by the State in varying degrees, in conjunction with organized social forces and influenced by the existing institutions.

Scope of Industrial Relations

It has been proved by the observations in industry, that when good relations prevail, the normal efficiency of workmen increases, work progress and the organisational growth advances. Organisations are benefited when they maintain good relations with their workmen, their unions and associations, other business contacts, neighbouring unions. It can help while negotiating with unions on matters related with wage agreements, annual bonus matters and other welfare activities too. All unions find such an atmosphere very much conducive when they deal within the organisation and with the other unions, their own counterparts working in other industry of officers, state machinery and legal systems. Overall approach to industrial relations should be so broad in nature that it should not be limited to the restricted use of bargaining alone.

While someone may speak about this subject with different terminology being used by many a managers, it is best known as 'employee-employer relations', relationship between 'workmen and management'. As also stated sometimes as "it is the kind of relationship which are necessary for corporation, coordination and fruitful working of men and women in the employment at any business activity".

The term industrial relations is more related and concerned with all the employees in an industry. It is this way of relation that is created at different levels within an organisation and outside business world by diverse groups of human being. These groups have variety of attitudes, values and behaviour patterns amongst themselves and in spite of this they try and keep in good books with each other. Thus to conclude we may say industrial relations mean:

(*a*) Relations between employees and employers.

(*b*) Relations between two distinct classes of workmen.

(*c*) Relations between two groups or two unions.

(*d*) Relations between two officers/managers or departments.

This process consists of both formal and informal relations by the members involved there. This process also continues to their homes normally after the duty hours and after retirement of one of the two. According to me following few major factors have direct influence on better or poor relations. They are:

Industrial Relations brought about drastic changes in the whole production system, working methods and human relations at workplace. Under the factory system of production, the owners provided the means of production, while workers supplied their labour. This ultimately led to the division of society into capitalist class who owned and controlled the means of production and working class which supplied the labour. In initial stages of industrial development mass production and division of labour enabled the capitalists to earn huge profits for investments, but the workers were exploited and made to work under unhealthy atmosphere for longer hours without holidays. As the workers were illiterate, untrained and unorganized, they could not receive proper remuneration from the employers. As there were no other employment opportunities available, the workers had to remain at the mercy of the capitalists.

During these days, Government followed the policy of non-intervention in day to day activities of economy (laissez faire policy). Hence the workers had to suffer heavily. At individual level, workers were very weak while contracting with very strong employers which led to the exploitation of the workers. As time passed, dissatisfaction among the workers increased and they became ready to protest. When workers realized that unless they unite, there is no survival, they formed Trade Unions to mobilize their labour power so as to bargain with employers on equal levels. Thus Trade Unions emerged in the area of collective relationship as organized bodies with the objective of protecting and promoting interests of the workers. At the same time, employer's unions or associations were also established to protect their own interests.

The inherent inequalities between the contracting parties in the employment process called for an intervention of the third party in the form of the Government to protect interests of both. The Government as the custodian of social welfare had to see that the economic needs of the people are satisfied through continuous flow of goods and services. Government passed several laws to regulate the relationship between the two parties.

Characteristic of Industrial Relations

The main features of industrial relations are:

(*i*) Industrial Relations are outcome of employment relationship in an industrial organization.

(*ii*) Industrial relations provide an opportunity to develop the skills and methods of adjusting to and cooperating with each other.

(*iii*) Industrial Relations system generates complex network of rules and regulations for the purpose of maintaining smooth and harmonious relations.

(*iv*) Government intervenes the industrial relations in social interests for regulating industrial relations through laws, rules, awards, agreements etc.

(*v*) The main parties involved in the process of industrial relations are:

- Employees and their organizations
- Employers and their associations
- Government.

(*vi*) Industrial relations are mainly the relations between the employers and employees.

(*vii*) The study of industrial relations also includes vital environmental issues like technology, social, economic and political environment, labour policy, attitude of the trade unions, workers as well as employers too.

(*viii*) Industrial Relations are dynamic in nature.

Objectives of Industrial Relations

The main objective of industrial relations system is to maintain and promote congenial industrial relations between employer and employees. The other objectives include:

(*i*) To promote economic welfare of the workers by way of providing better wages and other benefits.

(*ii*) To maintain the flow of production by reducing frequency of industrial conflicts.

(*iii*) To promote workers participation in management decision-making so as to get maximum cooperation of the workers.

(*iv*) To develop Trade Unions for uniting the workers and to improve the bargaining power of the workers.

(*v*) To improve workers strength so as to solve industrial problems through negotiations and consultation with management.

(*vi*) To establish two-way communication between workers and management in order to avoid misunderstanding and promote atmosphere of mutual trust and cooperation.

(*vii*) To work out schemes to promote creativity and cooperation to raise productivity and welfare of the members.

(*viii*) To promote and maintain healthy relations between management and workers.

(*ix*) To maintain industrial peace by way of preventing industrial disputes.

(*x*) To develop industrial democracy.

(*xi*) To avoid strikes, lock-outs, gheraos, go slow practices etc. by providing better wages and working conditions to the workers.

(*xii*) To protect interests of the workers and management by securing proper mutual understanding and goodwill between management and workers.

Importance of Healthy Industrial Relations

On account of increase in the size of organization and higher complexity of functioning of the management, the importance of industrial relations has been steadily increasing. In modern times, due to increase in sophistication of work methods and techno-based HRM policies, increased in literacy and knowledge of the workers etc. have give new and important dimensions to the industrial relations system.

In India, at present, around 33 per cent of labour force is employed in secondary and tertiary industries. Still industrial relations relating to this workforce affects not only the attitudes of unorganized workers but affects the economy as a whole. Hence the study of industrial relations stands out as an important aspect under Indian Industrial conditions.

The pattern of industrial relations of the organized sector of economy affects labour management relations in unorganized sector. Because, there are pressures from several groups on unorganized units to follow the employment and working conditions, fringe benefits etc. patterns of the organized sector.

The effect of the Trade Union activities are much wider on political system than on industry in India. Trade unions play a key role in elections of political parties. The unions supported by the political parties influence the legislative process through their effective lobbying activities. Even the Government consults with the local union's representatives while formulating various socio-economic as well as labour and employment policies. On account of their involvement in political activities in a wider scale, Indian Trade Unions have become a strong political force in India.

The pattern of industrial relations differs significantly in organized as compared to unorganized sector. In unorganized sector, where unionism is absent, worker's grievances are redressed by threatening of dismissal or physically beating in order to subside the industrial relations forever.

In India, since the Second-Five Year Plan, huge investment was made in public sector units (PSUs) to promote basic and key industries at a faster rate. So the workers in public sector get better wages, ideal working conditions, wider welfare facilities etc. hence, industrial relations in public sector units are most favourable while those in the private sector units are not much satisfactory, except few leading organizations. Since liberalization, exactly opposite trend is noticed as industrial relations are improving in private sector units, while they are worsening in public sector undertakings. This provides an interesting opportunity to study the dynamics of industrial relations in India.

The First-Five Year Plan has stated that an economy organized for planned production and distribution, aiming at the realization of social justice and the welfare of masses can function effectively only in an atmosphere of industrial peace.

Thus, harmonious industrial relations are necessary to attain and maintain higher productivity to fulfil the goals of our plans but also to bring about faster improvement in the standard of living of the masses in India. A developing country has to pay heavy costs for industrial conflicts. They not only affect labour, management and their organization, but also tend to make community still poorer. They lead to wastages of national resources, class conflicts, bitter mutual relations and adversely affect the progress of the nation.

It is often said that maintenance of congenial industrial relations particularly in a democratic society like India is not only significant task but also a highly complicated one. It is true, but there is no alternative for congenial industrial relations. Hence, at any cost, we have to maintain peace through healthy and sound industrial relations.

Good labour management relations is a necessary condition for achieving economic prosperity. But economic prosperity is based upon the existence of industrial democracy. Industrial democracy in turn facilitates collective bargaining, that helps in preserving good industrial relations.

Prerequisites for Successful Industrial Relations

In order to develop and maintain good industrial relations, it is necessary to have constructive and cooperative attitudes on the part of both the parties that is Management and the Unions. However, such an attitude depends upon the basic policies and procedures adopted by the organization for attaining and maintaining healthy industrial relations. It also depends upon responsibility. Both of them should have faith in the process of collective bargaining. The existence of strong, independent, democratic Trade Union for bargaining with management to protect interests of both the workers and organization is highly desirable.

In order to promote and maintain sound industrial relations, certain conditions are necessary as discussed below:

(1) Strong dynamic, democratic and responsible Trade Union is necessary to bargain on equal footing with the management and to protect interests of the workers.

(2) Sound and developed Employer's organizations are essential for laying down uniform personnel policies among various organizations and to protect interests of the employers.

(3) Spirit of cooperation among the Unions and Management is necessary so that all the differences between them can be settled through mutual negotiation and collective bargaining without intervention of third party. When the attempt fails to solve the issues through collective bargaining, then they may go for voluntary arbitration. Both the parties should avoid the adjudication procedure in order to maintain healthy relations.

(4) Supervisors should be trained so that they should be able to implement complex policies and programmes. This will help promote healthy human relations in the organization.

(5) Continuous review of industrial relations programmes is necessary to find out effectiveness of existing policy through evaluation and also for identifying and locating problems in the system. A system of regular data collection regarding labour turnover, absenteeism, job satisfaction, accidents, grievances, disputes etc. Should be developed in order not only to solve but also to predict the problems relating to industrial relations.

(6) Top management support is also necessary. For any programme to be effective, top management support is most necessary. Hence Industrial Relations programme cannot be an exception.

(7) Motivation of the employees is also desirable not only to produce larger output, but also to suggest new and practical ideas. The management should consider these ideas very seriously and if found acceptable should be adopted. When new ideas suggested by the employees are observed to be profitable to the organization. Then those workers should properly be rewarded and publicly acknowledged. In addition, the management should pay proper attention to satisfy the needs of the employees so that workers confidence in the good intentions of management will increase.

(8) Providing ideal environment is also useful to promote healthy industrial relations in the organization. An environment where the workers get maximum job satisfaction, assured bright future, providing his basic needs and attending and resolving grievances quickly may help to maintain industrial peace and harmony in the organization.

Origin and Growth of Industrial Relations in India

Industrial development on modern lines started in India around 1850s when Cotton Mills in Bombay, Jute Mills in

Kolkata were established. During early days, the relations between employees and employers were of the servant-master type. Majority of the workers were illiterate, unorganized and ignorant about their rights. Hence the workers were hired and fired at will be the employers. So Royal Commission on Labour observed, "before 1981, strikes were rare."

We shall discuss the Industrial Relations system in India under the following heads:

(*a*) The period before Independence (upto 1947)

(*b*) The period after Independence (1947-74)

(*c*) The period of Emergency and after (1975-1991)

(*d*) The period of New Economic Policy (1991 onwards)

Period before Independence

Although isolated disputes took place in India during eighties of the nineteenth century, these were hardly recorded. It was only after 1981 that they were considered as a serious feature of Indian economy. Before the World War-I strikes were rare as the workers were not organized and had passive outlook of life. However, after the end of the World War-I, relations between employers and workers became strained and industrial disputes became common on account of (*i*) growth of Trade Unions; (*ii*) Rise of labour leaders; (*iii*) awakening among the masses due to war; and (*iv*) Nationalist Movement.

The industrial Dispute Enquiry Committee (1921) reported that the:

(*a*) Bombay strikes took place without notice.

(*b*) Grievances were not clearly defined before going for strikes.

(*c*) The multiplicity of demands was brought forward when strike commenced.

(*d*) Lack of effective organization to give shape to the demands of the workers.

The established of ILO in 1919 led to the passing of the workmen's Compensation Act, 1923 and the Trade Unions Act, 1926 gave legal status to Trade Unions and granted them protection against criminal and civil suits in case of strikes. The Indian Trade Disputes Act, 1929 made a beginning of the interest of Government in the field of industrial unrest.

All India Trade Union Congress was the first Central Trade Union was established in 1920 still the trade Union Movement could not gather momentum to make unions strong enough to bargain with the employers on equal basis. The employers had the authoritarian attitude and they opposed the formation of Unions and treated it as a threat to their authority. During thc period, the Government was silent observer concentrating on preserving peace and order.

Strikes during 1920's were mainly due to:

1. The demand of workers for a share in the prosperity of the industry during the early boom period.
2. Resistance to reduction in wages during retrogression of the boom.
3. Political and labour leaders took interest in the management of their disputes.

During the period of Great depression (1930-1939) number of disputes increased to average 222 from 195 for the years 1921-29 but the average of number of workers involved and loss of mandays were lower.

The lower number of strikes during 1939-45 were 4000 involving 37 lakh workers and loss of mandays at 31.5 million. The workers demanded a share in the prosperity. Hence they were granted bonus and Dearness Allowance, but even then they were not satisfied as the increase in their income was lower than the rise in prices. Government tried to control dissatisfaction and strikes by Rules 81-A of the defence of India Rules. These rules provided for adjudication of disputes between employers and workers. This emergency measure continued to be a permanent feature of industrial relations system in India.

During 1946-47, the relations between labour and management were strained and number of strikes also increased. The number of Trade Unions also increased. The Indian National Trade Union Congress which is a new Central Union Organization was formed in 1947. A large number of labour laws were also formed during this period.

The Industrial Disputes Act, 1947 deals with the settlement of industrial disputes. At the State level, the Bombay Industrial Relations Act, 1946 provided for the statutory recognition of Trade Union.

It was the period during World War-II when the industrial development took place at a faster rate along with the diversification and growth in size and number of units. It also stimulated development of professional management but the management continued employer's authoritarian attitude towards labour rather than emphasizing human relations which was the need of the hour. The demand for higher wages and bonus were the main reasons giving rise to disputes in Cotton Textile, Woollen and Silk Industries, followed by Jute Mills, Railways and Mines.

Period after Independence (1947-74)

After war, the main objective was to attain faster growth of industrial sector which was thought to be the only solution to improve economic conditions of the people. The Government called a Tripartite Conference, where the Industrial Truce Resolution was adopted for maintaining industrial peace in India. In order to improve economic conditions of the workers and to protect their interests, the Government enacted several Acts covering various effects of industrial work and workers such as minimum Wages Act, 1948, the employees state Insurance Act, 1948, the Factories Act, 1948.

In the field of unionism, the process of disintegration during war years resulted in the establishment of three new

Central Trade Unions Organization during 1947-50. These are:

1. The Indian National Trade Union Congress (INTUC) led by Congress.
2. The Hind Mazdoor Sabha (HMS) led by socialists.
3. The United Trade Union Congress (UTUC) led by radical socialists.

During the period, cotton textile, Jute, Transport Industries suffered most on account of stoppages of work and increase in number of disputes.

Industrial Disputes in India

Year	No. of disputes	No. of workers involved	Mandays lost
1951	1071	6,91,321	38,18,928
1961	1357	5,11,860	49,18,755
1971	2752	1,38,937	1,65,45,636

The main causes of labour unrest were:

1. Feeling of Independence in the minds of employees which was considered as remedy for all their economic ills.
2. Tall promises of the congress leaders to promote significant improvement in wages and conditions of work.
3. Increase in communistic influence on the thinking of workers.
4. Continuous rise in the cost of living.
5. Feeling of insecurity into retrenchment and unemployment.
6. Political dominance of labour leadership.
7. Employer's apathy to labour problems.
8. State's time consuming process of dealing with labour problems.

As a result of the Code of Discipline, which was evolved in 1958, the number of strikes during 1958-60 declined although the number of mandays lost increased significantly.

During 1968-69, the number of disputes increased due to sharp rise in prices, recession in some industries leading to retrenchment, lay off and closure. As Industrial Relations climate continued to deteriorate when workers adopted Gheraos and Bandhs in 1970-73.

The Period of Emergency and After

During the period of Emergency (1975-77) there was declining trend in industrial conflicts, although industrial relations climate could not change. Employers declared lockouts which resulted into loss of more mandays than strikes.

During post-emergency period, the trend was reserved and situation started deteriorating especially in the states of West Bengal and Maharashtra. It was described as a result of out bust of the rigorous and excesses suffered by the workers during emergency period. The workers discontent went on accumulating during emergency because of the rejection of their routine grievances and the virtual suspension of trade union activities. During 1979-84, there was increasing trend in the loss of mandays. In January, 1982, the longest strike in textile Industry was staged by Datta Sawant, a militant Trade Union leader, in which more than 2.5 lakh workers of 60 textile mills in Bombay were involved in the strike. The loss of wages was estimated are Rs. 300 crores to workers and loss of Rs. 200 crores to the mills and the production of cloth worth Rs. 2000 crores was averagely hit. The loss on account of strike was 41.40 million mandays, however, the strike failed miserably making workers to suffer most. Due to sever financial crisis, several mills were closed and 13 mills were transferred under Government control. Since 1976, the mandays lost on account of lockouts are reflecting rising trend.

The period of New Economic Policy (1991 onwards)

In 1991, the Government of Indian declared the New Economic Policy where a series of Industrial, Fiscal and Trade Reforms were announced. It was believed that the structural changes would reduce growing inertia deeply rooted in Indian economy on account of mismanagement and emphasis on unrealistic economic policies over more than four decades. The new economic policy has generated new business environment where the private sector is liberated from excessive controls by the Government. Industries are freed from tariffs and custom duties. The threshold limit of MRTP has been removed. FERA has been relaxed and foreign capital could be utilized effectively.

In order to maintain harmonious industrial relations under changed environment requires that all the players have to work sincerely to make the system effective. On account of increase in hostility and volatility of business environment, it becomes difficult to formulate and implement suitable strategies.

In this context, *Memoria and Others* have suggested the following courses of actions:

1. Adoption of more harmonious organizational design by doing away with mechanistic one.
2. Introducing plans for career growth of workforce.
3. Achieving employee growth and minimizing their obsolescence through a system of regular training.
4. Rationalizing workforce through internal transfers, accommodating obsolete misfit workers in sister/ family concerns.
5. Refraining form unfair labour practices.
6. Nurturing trust between the Union and Management.
7. Eliciting Union support in change of Management and organizational functioning.

8. Inculcating of proper work culture through humanization and personalization of management.

Both, Management and workers have to realize that their interests are interrelated. Hence, instead of depending on outside help from Government or political party, they should help themselves wherein lies the solution of the problems of industrial conflict. A free and frank communication between workers and Management at all levels, mutual confidence and faith, development of collective bargaining and willingness to abide by the agreements entered into, a recognition of growing strength of Trade Unions and their ability to get better working conditions, welfare amenities and higher wages for their members, better labour-management relations and determination that all the differences and disputes must be settled voluntary arbitration, these are the 'sine quo of a new era of industrial relations.

Evolution of Industrial Relations in India

Industrial relations assume a unique role in the establishment and maintenance of industrial democracy. In a narrow sense, it refers to labour relations only. *i.e.,* relations between management (representing owners) and labour unions (representing organized workers). In a broad sense, it includes employee relations, labour relations, public relations, customer relations etc. In India, industrial relations means labour relations only. Industrial relations in a wider sense cover three types of relations:

Personnel Relations

They refer to the relations of management with individual employees, *i.e.,* management of workers within the plant, such activities include, for *e.g.,* selection, training rating, promotion, wage administration, welfare, safety, health etc.

Labour Relations

They describe the relations of management with a group of employees, especially collective bargaining or contract between the employer and the Trade Union. In the modern industrial set-up, both employers as well as employees, are fully organized and, therefore, labour relations with management usually represent importance of collective bargaining, *i.e.*, agreement through voluntary negotiations, conciliation and arbitration on all vital labour problems. Industrial relations covering personnel relations and labour relations describe all activities of management, by which it can secure enthusiastic and willing co-operation of human resources to maximize productivity and efficiency of the enterprise as a whole.

Public Relations

As business enterprise is a special organization and as management is a social process, relations of the company with outsiders, *e.g.*, suppliers, consumers, financiers, government and the general public, play an important role in building up a bright public image and market reputation of the company. Every enterprise in a free market or competitive economy must consider public opinion while conducting its business. Public opinion is a vital force which can make the future prospects of the enterprise particularly, in the private sector of the economy. In the heat of daily conflict, the community is the most dominant partner which cannot be conveniently forgotten by management and labour the two disputing parties. A business enterprise, as a social institution, must establish cordial and ensure peaceful relations with the public at large. Only then, it can ensure public welfare and social justice to all. A change of attitude and a change of heart of both will be the sine-quo-non for the maintenance of industrial peace.

Industrial relations are shaped by three agencies: Such as (1) Management; (2) Labour Unions; (3) Government through legislation. If industrial relations are cordial and harmonious, we can have: (1) Maximum productivity; (2) maximum wage rates; (3) Maximum dividends; (4) Maximum plough back of profits; and (5) Lower prices and better quality of products. In short, both industry and economy will enjoy all round prosperity. Low productivity, Trade Union rivalry, lack of education and training, employer's hostility, political interference, depressed living standards due to poverty and ignorance, seriously affect the health development of industrial relations in a developing and populous country like India. The history of industrial relations in India has been characterized by frequent occurrences of disputes between the workers and the employers. In absence of strong Trade Unions, majority of employers have tried to exploit the workers. Whenever the orders organized themselves into a powerful union and resorted to collective bargaining, the employer conceded to their demands but not always without resort to a stoppage of work. This is borne out by the statistics of industrial disputes.

It is seen that between 1951-64 on an average, 53.26 lakhs of working days have been lost every year. It means heavy losses to all concerned, workers suffer loss of wages, employers lose profits on the production. It means a reduction in the output of goods and services. Frequent occurrences of such disputes tend to embitter relations between employers and employees and to lower the productive efficiency of industry.

Effects of Social, Political, Economic and Legal Changes on Industrial Relations

Effect of Political changes on Industrial Relations

The effect of the political changes manifests itself in the form of changes in the legal framework of industrial relations. The political changes influences structural changes in the basic framework of industrial relations through statutes. In the process of rule making, the two parties, the workers and employers/management, exhibit their strength but learn to adjust, and the government agencies, with regulative powers at their disposal, play a decisive role in shaping industrial relations.

Effect of Economic Changes on Industrial Relations

The effect of economic changes on industrial relations may be assessed with regard to a number of factors, such as market influences inflationary pressures. Level of employment or unemployment, the tax structure, that is taxes on income, both personal and corporate. The overall situations of rising prices influences significantly the process of wage negotiations and settlements. The demand fluctuations in the product markets results in uncertainties in factor markets, including an adverse impact on the requirement and price of labour. The macro level position of employment in the region/industry either helps or acts as a constraints on the collective bargaining of workers. The nature of personal income taxation is a deciding factor in the context of negotiations for wage revisions.

Effect of Social Changes on Industrial Relations

The change in the social status of the worker is reflected in the change in labour management relations and also in the management's attitude to trade unions. Trade unions now, due to impact of social change, have been accepted as an essential part of the apparatus of the industrial and economic administration of the country. Now, the worker is no longer a mere factor of production but is regarded as a responsible partner in the industry.

Effect of Legal Changes on Industrial Relations

Due to legal changes in the country's judiciary system, there is significant impact on industrial relations. The worker, now, is not mere commodity, he has been given equal status by the law in the industrial relations along with the employer. Several laws and rules have been enacted to protect the workers from injustice. The management/employer has to consider all these factors to maintain sound industrial relations.

Various Attitudes towards the Industrial Relations

Psychological Attitude

Psychologists argue that the problems of industrial relations have their origin in the perceptions of the management, unions and the workers. Mason Harie studies behaviour of two different groups of union leaders and managers. To carry out the test, a photograph of ordinary angry middle aged person was used for rating by both groups. Both groups rated the same photograph differently. The union leaders described the person in the photograph as manager while managers described is as Trade Union leader. On the basis of his study, Harie concluded that:

1. The general impression about a person radically differs when he is a representative of management and then as a representative of workers.

   Thus a person behaves differently in both these capacities.

2. The management and labour see each other as less dependable.
3. The management and labour are more interested in the protection of self-interests rather than management considering view of the labour and labour and labour from the point of view of the management.
4. Management and labour, while thinking for others feel that the other party is not able to appreciate properly the interpersonal relations and emotional characteristics.

This difference arises because of their individual perceptions. The conflict between labour and management arises because they perceive each other's behaviour negatively and even the honest intention of the other party is looked upon with suspension. In most of the industrial conflicts, interests of the parties, personalities of actors in the system, neglected needs of power, prestige, recognition, motives etc. along with interpersonal and inter-group relations lead to the imbalances and conflicts in the system.

Socio-Ethical Attitude

According to this approach, individual relations have ethical angle along with sociological base. Healthy industrial relations call for realization of both the parties, labour and management, their moral responsibility of achieving organizations goals through mutual cooperation and greater understanding of the problems faced by each other. The study group of the National Commission on labour observed that the industrial relations exist within social, economic and political structures of society. So they should be studies in the context of overall institutional and ideological goals of democratic socialism and economic growth. The group emphasized that "The goal of labour-management relations may be stated as maximum productivity"—Leading to rapid economic development, adequate understanding among employers, workers and government of each other's role in industry, commitment to industry and individual way of life on the part of labour and management, sound unionism, efficient, institutionalized mechanism for handling industrial disputes and willingness among parties to cooperate as partners in the industrial system.

V.V. Giri has emphasized the collective bargaining and mutual negotiations between employers and employees for the settlement of industrial disputes. Voluntary efforts should be given preference over compulsory arbitration. Giri held the view that compulsory adjudication cuts at the very root of the Trade Union organizations. Thus, Giri's bargaining, voluntary arbitration and not compulsory adjudication. Thus it puts ethical pressure on parties for maintenance of healthy industrial relations through peaceful settlement of disputes.

Systems Attitude

John Dunlop developed the systems approach to industrial relations. The approach is helpful to study industrial relations as it emphasizes on: (*i*) participants in the process; (*ii*) environmental forces; and (*iii*) the output. It also studies the interrelationships among different aspects of industrial relations. His model can be explained as follows:

The main characteristics of the systems approach are:

(a) ***Participants in the System:*** Dunlop states that there are three major participants: (*i*) workers and their organizations; (*ii*) Management and its representatives; and (*iii*) Specialized Government Agencies such a 'Labour Courts'. These interact within social and economic framework.

(b) ***An Ideological Linking:*** According to Dunlop, an ideology is asset of ideas and beliefs commonly held by the actors that help to bind or integrate the system as a single entity. The ideology regulates the relations among the parties.

(c) ***The Context or Environment:*** It is the environment under which the participants interact. In the context of industrial relations, Dunlop identifies three types of environments.

(*i*) Technological characteristics of workshop or technological subsystem.

(*ii*) Economic system covering market and economic constraints.

(*iii*) Political subsystem: Conflicts arise when the parties are less mature, power conscious and aggressive.

(d) ***The Output:*** It is the result of the interaction of the actors in the system which gives rise to the network of rules and regulations, labour policies of Government, labour agreements etc. that facilitate fair deal to workers.

Effects of (Sound) Industrial Relations on Management

An economy organized for planned production and distribution, aiming at the realization of social justice and welfare of the masses can function effectively only in an atmosphere of industrial peace. If the twin objectives of rapid national development and increased social justice are to be achieved, there must be harmonious relationship between management and labour. The impact of good industrial relations on production may be seen from the following facts:

Reduces Industrial Disputes

Good industrial relations reduce the industrial disputes. Disputes are reflections of the failure of basic human urges or motivations to secure adequate satisfaction or expression which are fully cured by good industrial relations. Strikes, lockouts, go-slow, tactics, gherao and grievances are some of the reflections of industrial unrest which do not spring up in an atmosphere of industrial peace. It helps promoting cooperation and increasing production.

High Morale

Good industrial relations improve the morale of the employees. Employees work with great zeal with the feeling in mind that the interest of employer and employees is one and the same, *i.e.* to increase production. Every worker feels that he is a co-owner of the industry. The employer in his turn must realize that the gains of industry are not for him alone but they should be shared equally and generously with his workers. In other words, complete unity of thought and action is the main achievement of industrial peace. It increase the place of workers in the society and their ego is satisfied. It naturally affects production because a mighty co-operative efforts alone can produce great results.

Mental Revolution

The main object of industrial relation is a complete mental revolution of workers and employers. The industrial peace lies ultimately in a transformed outlook on the part of both. It is the business of leadership in the ranks of workers, employees and Government to work out a new relationship is consonance with a spirit of true democracy. Both should think themselves as partners of the industry and the role of workers in such a partnership should be recognized. On the other hand, workers must recognize employers authority. It will naturally have impact on production because they recognize the interest of each other.

New Programmes

New programmes for workers development are introduced in an atmosphere of peace such as training facilities, labour, labour welfare facilities etc. it increase the efficiency of workers resulting in higher and better production at lower costs.

Reduced Wastage

Good industrial relations are maintained on the basis of co-operation and recognition of each other. It will help increase production, wastage's of man, material and machines are reduced to the minimum and thus national interest is protected. Thus from the above discussion it is evident that good industrial relation is the basis of higher production with minimum cost and higher profits. It also results in increased efficiency of workers. New and new projects are introduced for the welfare of the workers and to promote the morale of the people at work.

Reasons/Causes of Poor Industrial Relations between Employer and Employee

Causes of Poor Industrial Relations: The new industrial set up has given birth to the capitalistic economy which divided the industrial society into two groups of labour and capitalists.

The interests of these two groups are not common which creates industrial disputes. The main causes of industrial disputes may be classified into four groups.

(*i*) Economic

(*ii*) Managerial

(*iii*) Political

(*iv*) Others.

Now we shall discuss these cases as follows:

Economic Causes

Really, the most common causes of industrial disputes are economic causes. These are as follows:

(*a*) ***Wages:*** The demand for wage increase is the prime most cause of the industrial disputes. A large number of strikes are being organized to raise a voice against the rise in prices and cost of living. The real wages of the workers decline faster and they feel dissatisfied with their present employments and struggle for the improvement in wages. By having a cursory glance on the history of industrial dispute; it becomes clear that cause of most of the industrial disputes was wages. The Indian employer have no clear cut and enlightened wage policy. Most of the industrial disputes were the result of a demand for higher wages.

(*b*) ***Dearness Allowance and Bonus:*** Increase in cost of living was the main cause of the demand of dearness allowance by the workers to equate their wages with the rise of prices. Bonus also play an important role as a cause of industrial dispute. Both the quantum and the method of bonus payment had led to a number of disputes. There is an increasing feeling among the workers that they should have a greater share in the profits of the concern and this fact has not been recognized by the employees and non-acceptance of this fact has been a source of friction among employers and employees.

(c) ***High Industrial Profits:*** During and after the world wars, prices of the commodities went up and the industrialists earned a huge profit. In order to get share in the prosperity of industry it naturally led to the resentment on their part. The increased profits also led to the demands of higher wages and bonus. Now in the changing world, concept of labour has changed considerable. They think themselves as a partner of the industry and demand their share in the profits.

(d) ***Working Condition and Working Hours:*** The working conditions in Indian industries are not hygienic. There is not ample provision of water, heating, lighting, safety etc. working hours are also greater. The demand of palatable working conditions and shorter hours of work are also responsible for labour disputes.

(e) ***Modernization and Automation of Plant and Machinery:*** The attempt to modernization and introduction of automatic machinery to replace labour has been the major cause of disputes of India. Workers go on strike off and on to resist rationalization and automation. A strike in cotton textile industry in Kanpur in 1955 is an example of such disputes. Workers in Life Insurance Corporation went on strike recently against introducing computers in the corporation.

(f) ***Demand for Other Facilities:*** Demand for other facilities for meeting out their basic needs such as medical, education, housing etc. encourage the workers to resort to direct action because such facilities were denied by the employers.

Managerial Causes

These causes include autocratic managerial attitude and defective labour policies etc.

(a) ***Denial of Recognition to Trade Unions:*** Failure on the part of the employer to recognize the trade unions or to recognize rise the rival union of representation, insult of trade union leaders by the employers are some of the examples of autocratic managerial attitude worth mentioning as the causes of industrial disputes. The attitude of employers towards the labour association had never been sympathetic. They want to divide them and rule.

(b) ***Defective Recruitment Policies:*** The recruitment practices in Indian industries are defective. Recruitment is generally made by the contractors who exploit the workers and suppress their individuality. The defective promotion, demotion, transfer and placement policies encourage dissatisfaction among workers.

(c) ***Irregular Lay-off and Retrenchment:*** Lay off and retrenchment are reasons to be mentioned for encouraging industrial disputes. Indian employers follow the policy of hire and fire. As a matter of practice workers are not permanent for a pretty long time to deprive them of their legitimate rights.

(d) ***Defiance of Agreements and Codes:*** The employers regularly defy the provisions of collective bargaining agreements and code of conduct and code of discipline with a view to harass or exploit the employees and just encourage strife.

(e) ***Defective Leadership:*** Inefficient leadership is also one of the causes of disputes. Leadership from the management and from the workers and quite incompetent to induce the workers to get them worked. Defective management leadership ignored the labour problems and inefficient labour leadership could not co-ordinate the efforts of their fellow members, so disputes arise.

(f) ***Weak Trade Unions:*** In our country trade unions are weak. According to labour commission (1969) only 24 per cent of all workers were members of trade unions. In some undertakings, there is no union and in some other undertakings, there are more than one union. Both the situations weaken the trade union movement. The workers in non-union undertaking resort to direct action instead of collective bargaining which can be a better course of action if there is a proper trade union.

Political Causes

The political environment also influenced the work environment in the industry.

Influence of Politicians: Political parties or political ideologies governed the trade unions movement in India. All the four national unions are affiliated to one or the other political ideologies. The political workers misuse the industrial workers to serve the political purpose and arrange strikes, gheraos, etc.

Other Causes

Apart from the reasons mentioned above these are several other reasons of industrial disputes worth-mentioning here such as symphatetic strike etc.

Factors for Maintaining sound industrial relations:

(*a*) There is a full acceptance by management of the collective bargaining process and of unionism as an institution. The company considers strong union as an asset to the management.

(*b*) The union fully accepts private ownership and operations of the industry; it recognizes that the welfare of its members depends upon the successful operations of the business.

(*c*) The union is strong, responsible and democratic.

(*d*) The company stays out of the internal affairs of the union it does not seek to alienate the worker's allegiance to their union.

(*e*) Mutual trust and confidence exists between the parties. There have been no serious ideological incompatibilities.

(*f*) Neither party to bargaining adopts legalistic approach to the solution of the problem of relationship.

(*g*) Negotiation should be problem-entered. More time is spent on the day-to-day problem than on defining abstract principles.

(*h*) There are wide spread union management consultations and highly developed information sharing.

(*i*) Grievances are settled promptly in the local plant, wherever possible. There is flexibility and informality within the procedure.

(*j*) The environment factors do not by themselves cause peace but they create conditions to develop it. The attitudes and policies of the parties, the personality of the leaders and their techniques, bring about good relations.

Factors Responsible for Problem Emergence

Organisation Structure

Companies those existed till 1960 mostly relied on centralised system of organisation structures, where the orders from the top were passed on correctly and complied properly without any resistance. This set up did not encourage enterprise of initiative on part of staff. However, this did not help the companies in a very positive manner and some other companies shifted to free, more decentralised systems, where persons were encouraged to keep open thoughts and participate in all the process of decision-making at the top levels. Often decisions related with workmen were discussed with the representatives of the workforce, may be through a committee appointed by the workmen.

In the organisational structure there are two patterns followed by employees themselves as 'formal and informal organisations', when the formal positions of authorities of employees are followed depending upon the nature of work, urgency of task and also designation of the persons involved therein. Organisation structure also elaborates about the present status of a position, a Manager or an officer and his area of work, his authority and the functions handled by him. This further tells us about the scope of his duties as regards achievement of the results and in some cases his power to use his authority as regards the financial commitments and expenditure for which he is held responsible for.

The advantage of having a well designed organisation structure is that it reduces ambiguity while working in the department. Most of the persons dealing with him know his area and also his power to take decisions and implementation limits when certain decisions are taken by some of his subordinates, or actions suggested by some of his assistants. It is only when some decisions are taken and implemented successfully for the benefits of the people and the department in general that people start believing on the capacity of the officer or the manager. Mere talking and announcing the prove that he has a capacity to take decision and also freedom to implement those.

Every company and its department has to function in a given set of direction towards the organisational goals set by the top management. Such goals are narrated by the seniors and then passed on to the others working there. Now it is the duty of those connected with the implementation of these goals to formulate some definite systems, procedures and rules for all the persons to follow and thus help achieve the targeted goals. Thus while working within these rules and set procedures persons have to develop their own set of behaviour and accordingly deal with all human beings while meeting the duties, responsibilities and taking appropriate actions, which sometimes may be or may not be favourable to all. This is a direct reason which admires or destroys the relations in working.

All human beings like things to happen in their favour and if these do not, then a bad taste is carried by them throughout their future relations with each other. This sometimes does not stop at that level, but spreads to other unconnected persons and departments also. Sometimes the matter becomes so serious that the issues are taken up by the elected representatives of the workmen and then discussed amongst their senior members or office bearers further to be taken up at higher authority for arriving at some solution. Petty matters like sanctioning of leave, passing of travelling bills, payments of overtime, transfer of goods from one department to other, non-availability of company owned vehicles to the elected representatives and many others cause ill feeling and this leads to our industrial relations.

Mutual Trust

This is another delicate subject area where both the parties involved are very much concerned with while dealing with each other. Right from the earlier days and ages, we have been told by our parents and also seen the practices of our earlier rulers not to believe our friends, subordinates so easily, unless there are minimum number of occasions and events when such a relation has proved with desired results, mostly in our favour. It is seen in the companies managed by senior leaders, that they have been brought up with such a training only and thus they have developed the way of not believing any of their sub-ordinates. They keep asking reports about one person from the other and thus try to keep track of things in the department. This may be a thumb rule called 'Divide and Rule' followed and practiced for years together by our earlier rulers, who taught us so many things and these as the most important ones.

As often noticed by people at all level, it is this degree of mutual trust at all levels which makes the whole lot of difference in maintaining the relations. We speak to many persons, we make commitments to many, we promise many things to many persons and probably forget about them in near future, may be some of them have no relevance or these are not very important. Do we all the time keep writing all of them so that in future we do not land up in trouble?

When things are of minor nature and of his place in the working one should not be keeping those in mind and keep nagging about it to the higher ups. But this does not happen and most people in the organisation keep remembering only small items and continue bothering their neighbours, it at all the time, so as to make things better and feel better.

As far as an organisation is concerned, mutual trust is a philosophy followed and practiced by the seniors and top level managers, which can turn the table and the scenes would be totally different. Organisations necessarily design such procedures that there is always a second check by some senior so that things do not prove to be wrong or against the interest of the company. This is mainly because the seniors are not sure about the mental and/or physical capacity of their staff about the successful completion of any task assigned to them. Seniors have developed this thinking from their previous experience of the same staff or the staff employed earlier, who are no longer in the service now. Similarly, staff may not be capable of doing things in a proper manner and not according to the instructions given to them by the seniors. Sometimes we find people do not take any initiative in the work and thus are little careless in performing.

This idea of disbelief or second check is percolated right from the top to the bottom most level and thus continues further into homes of people right up to their wives and children. Managers should think now in the current century about this root cause of poor industrial relations, since it is alrealy late when we think of entering into the 21st century.

Some basic questions like the ones given below should be

asked while asking someone to perform any work, or handling over some assignment.

1. Is it necessary to show doubts about all the employees all the time?
2. Are we trying to build enough safety nets around us? Around each other in the same department?
3. Are we planning for every eventuality and exceptional situation?
4. Is it not a time to revise some procedures that may be creating some mistrust in minds of the staff or workmen?

According to me mistrust is the real cause of creation of poor industrial relations and hence it should be seen in that perspective by all those concerned with people and are given the responsibility of working with the help of people. In a way this appears to be so analytical thinking that total organisational structure if based upon mutual trust would look different, work on different footings and shall certainly produce different results.

Features of Workplace

Workplace here means the geographical location of the company or the industry. Often it is found that the atmosphere in any industrial estate is caught up suddenly without any delay by the workmen and their relations get to worst. In Maharashtra, for that matter anywhere in the industrial estates declared by the government, some part of some estate gets polluted by certain unwarranted behaviour of some workmen and their relations with their owners or management get strained. The reflection of this atmosphere is immediately spread over to the other parts of the estate, district or the state.

Some of the backward districts, for that matter every state has few even today, are not in a position to provide any employment opportunity to a lot of young people – educated or craftsmen—leaving all of them to accept any job that comes on their way to make two ends meet and survive. Some remote places are still out of reach of irrigation water and though some families own sufficient land they are unable to cultivate it and thus have to be dependent upon other source of earning like any job or service.

Based upon the basic law of economics of 'Demand and supply', the wage and salary structure offered to all such easily available people is obviously low. Another reason for low wages may be the economic condition of the company itself, for which many factors are responsible, which shall be taken up for discussions later.

Due to the remote geographical location some companies find it difficult to attract good and trained manpower. In such cases the companies, as a policy, decide to offer many other facilities like residential quarters, recreation facilities etc. To some selected group of employees, who may demand any negotiate such extra times on the pay scale at the time of negotiations. Once the families also stay together with the workmen, officers, all of them get assured about the safety and security aspects and thus can surely concentrate more on their job.

Remote location, has some other advantages like mental stability and financial stability achieved by their employees. Since the organization provides for anything and everything for all of them, no one really is interested to leave the job and jump upon to another, however lucrative it may be. Persons think over such offers and calculate all possible combinations of income and expenditure statements and decide to stay there, almost permanently.

I was associated with such few companies during my assignments of study and training and I have noticed this pattern of life. These days, most of the companies, with a view to stay competitive, look for some economic benefits like tax holidays, benefits of backward areas etc. and prefer to go a little further from cities. They establish plans and residential colonies and thus make all arrangements like hospitals, schools, playground, hostel facilities etc., so that the employees children are placed comfortable and assure of the best possible education. Some large scale organisations situated near places like Kalyan (C. Railway, junction), Patalganga (Dist. Raigad) and Solapur, Ahmednagar, Satara etc. all have provisions states above and people there are living a better and certainly comfortable pattern of life than their counterparts in urban, crowded cities. I had the opportunities to visit these places and see the set ups of large organisations like Reliance, Jindals etc. and see for myself how these companies are comfortable with there highly devoted workforce.

There are examples of few generations being in service with a company near Satara and Solapur and people there have no sour feelings. There are other examples of people thinking of living such an atmosphere just for the attraction of the present day changes in the pay scales, offered by most of the newly opened joint venture multinational companies to their staff, all working in cities and urban places. Some of them took some hasty decisions and after sufficient rethinking decided to rejoin the company, where they have worked for few decades earlier.

On this background, I have also seen some remote places in other states where all these facilities are not provided, probably it not possible for those companies to do that. Some industrial estates in spite of being close to main cities are kept physically away and not provided with basic amenities for the workmen.

Taking the advantages of provisions in the laws, certain companies have established their plans within five kilometers from a city so that they do not have to provide any residential and other facilities and as such there staff has to travel all the way to the place of work daily and incure heavy expenditure in conveyance.

Human beings, being social animals, prefer to stay close to their communities and perform all the activities along with their relatives, friends. They also believe that the basic purpose of their working and earning is to provide basic living and education to their children so that their future is secured and safe. Every person has also a dream of earning sufficient for himself and for his family first and then make enough provisions for the future requirements, may be after retirement. With these thoughts in the mind most of the employees prefer to have all the above amenities near the place of work so that they work in a calm state of their minds with maximum savings for the future.

Financial Freedom

With starting of early seventies of this century, we find there has been a swift change in the entire family set up. Younger generations like to be free and separate from their parents and like to establish themselves. Thus young ones in the family complete their basic education and start looking for a job in cities. There they achieve total freedom but they are still dependent upon the companies for their monthly earnings and thus keep working at the place for the period till they come across a better, lucrative offer. Financial crisis is one thing that crumbles any person to agree to any working condition, terms of contracts and work environments, without any sour feelings. Most of the large size families who have only one/two sources of income prefer a stabilised service and insist the same on the minds of their children. These large size families have greater liability on account of education of all the members of the family, their set up and well being and hence some of the members also prefer not to change the job frequently for minor gains.

There is another category of large size family, where number is large but the earning members are limited. This results in low standard of living for all the members. Thus members prefer a gainfull employment as early as possible, leaving higher education, or after completing a small craftsmen's course sufficient enough to secure a job some where. This family is always on look out for early availability of an additional member ready for earning and as soon as an opportunity is seen, a job is secured and continued for lifelong, under whatever conditions and environments. Most of these families have a foremost priority of setting a permanent source of earning and better their standard of living.

Employees belonging to these categories keep working for years together and hardly think of changing the jobs, by maintaining good relations with their staff, officers and in general with every one around.

Mental Frame

Some of the families either in business or service, have develop a set mental frame about the life pattern of their children and have accordingly nurtured them through a way, right from their childhood that once grown all of them start thinking about the set, secured, safe and risk free routine life. Such populations find themselves comfortable in the service/job at the locations described above. Their nature and way of life appears to be contented as far as the achievements are concerned, without much ambition of doing something different than others. Some lucky once may prefer and obtain jobs in government departments and start a similar life pattern. It is also observed by me that the average present age of the employees in companies providing all amenities around, is very high as compare with the average age of employees working in urban set ups. This higher age group employees feel more secured to be in one job for a lifetime, a concept very much liked and practiced by the industries in Japan.

We find many a cases in India too when we look around at the generation which was in job and working at government services, till 1970-80. These persons valued such a pattern of working at ONE EMPLOYER for a longer period as a 'sign of settlement in the life'.

People who see some opportunities around, decide for a changeover and do so, even without consulting their parents. This is possible in cities and urban places because of presence of many a large and small size business houses, and the emergence of risk taking behaviour by the new generations. Though overall percentage of this risk taking population is very low, their existence cannot be ignored now a days. According to them changing job and the salary slabs is the key word for their progress in the life. This class of employees does not very much bother and worry about maintaining good industrial relations.

Education

There are many persons who are capable of learning and achieving higher education in the life but they do not get enough support and the conducive atmosphere at their homes. Most of the families described under Sr No. 4 and 5 do not have inclination towards higher education. The senior member do not aspire for any recognizable qualifications for themselves and nor insist for it for their children. Such populations when comes to industry has no much choice but to accept any type of work and start earning.

Since financial capacity is low this results into flow educational achievements also. In some cases we also find that basically for families, their children have low mental capacity of absorption and thus prefer to stay away from any burden of normal education. Often they cannot gather enough courage to openly tell their parents, but prove the same by their annual examination result sheet, that one day the parents decide not to press hard and allow such children to opt for any short course and look forward to their earning time. This low educated employee-groups then do not have capacity to think over any serious matter or matters concerning about the decisions pertaining to their personal affairs. They are always dependent upon someone else to work for them and guide them through any hard and difficult decisions. Matters related to their job, duties, nature of work, place of work, overtime working, uniform, canteen facilites etc. all are decided by their elected members on their behalf with the management company. This what happen in the process of bargaining.

In all such cases elected members also know that these workmen are dependent upon them and are in need of a leader to work for them. The leader is also sure that these workmen have little choice of work in the life and they would stick around with present job for years together. It becomes imperative for the leaders to work and satisfy them so as to keep their own position always in demand, years after years. In India even after several years of industrial development we have large number of workmen in this category, who leave the present and the future in the hands of their leaders, since they have no other way to handle their grievances and demands.

There is yet another category of workmen, who are unaware about the importance of learning and further education once they get into any job. For them getting a job is in itself a destination or full stop. Some others decide right in the beginning of their career about the level to which they would want to rich and accordingly safe their own low standards about the education levels. Such a standard is obviously low or insufficient when compared with others, but no one else can motivate a person than himself, is the rule of the game everywhere. Thus this category also prefers to remains under the shelters of elected members all the time. For them whatever is told and explained by the elected members is true and the last word in the life or any matter related to their work, salary, increment, annual benefits etc.

In India this phenomenon is commonly present everywhere because of many reasons like poverty, large size of families etc. The situation is further worsen by some earlier political leaders, who never wanted our people to be educated. They were afraid that once workmen learn and get to know many things, they may further not come to the leaders for any assistance. Thus leaders themselves are to certain extent responsible for this situation today, though the picture is fast changing during last twenty odd years.

Market Position

As agreed by every one, companies need to have a sound market position as regards the sale of their products and an assured income flow, from which the management would satisfy the demands of the workmen to establish good industrial relations.

But there is a vicious circle. If there is no assured income from the sales of the products, the revenue gets affected and to that extent the capacity of the companies to spend on the normal as well as extra facilities for the workmen. Market leadership can be made possible by the high quality of the products together with reasonable price tag and timely deliveries to meet the demands of the customers. These facets of any business are easily achieved only if the workmen are educated enough to understand the importance of these facets, either on their own or through continuous learning or training imparted by their management.

As most economists put it to us through articles in the newspapers, market share of any given product is a highly volatile item on the agenda of all the marketing departments of the companies, though it cannot be decided by them but purely lies in the hands of their customers, their changing choice, capacity to buy and craze for new items all the time.

Market share of a product shows a cyclical trend and every industry has to pass through this. All years of the business are not same, with uneven bounces and no one can predict about it. Industrial relations concept may not agree with this.

We talk about future benefits and assurances from the management, but never understand that it is beyond the scope of anybody's guess to decide the next year's sales and revenue. How any one can promise certain amount of annual benefits? On what grounds that may be adhered to when basic sales volume is undecided?

Sometimes organisations find it difficult to deliver their products in time to their customers, for the reasons beyond their control—petty disruptions like transporters' strike, floods, booking not available and so on. But members of the bodies of the workmen organisations try and argue on the basis of the net production volumes while demanding their production incentives, irrespective of thc fact that finished goods are still lying in the factory premises, due to some of the above reasons.

Workmen and their members should know and understand such constraints often faced by the management and extend their co-operation towards the cause of good industrial relations specially in a period of crisis.

Some companies face a different kind of problem of low margin on the overall revenue earned by it. This volume of low margin is the sum of surplus funds available for distribution amongst its shareholders, workmen etc. This margin is necessarily the difference between the sales price of the products [SP] minus the cost of production [CP]. Taking into account all the constraints to management and other limitations posed by the system in which the company is operating, this margin percentage is decided by the price and cost of production ratio. Since fixing of price is not within the scope of companies, they may have to try their best and contain the cost of production as much as they can.

There is another reason when this margin falls to a minimum level decided by the company. In a competitive market when your competitor tries to offer a price much lower than yours, you wonder, how is that possible. Customer, if has decided to place the order with the lowest price offer, he would certainly awards the contract to him and you get suffered. There are many a companies who suffer on this account now a days, may be due to entry of many new and better products in the market. Every new product tries to have its own share and to retain that, it tries all possible ways and means.

A boiler manufacturing company recently had to accept an order at Rs. 2.65 crore against its quotation of Rs. 3.8 crore because of stiff competition and other market forces operating at the time of negotiations. This company is in the business for last 25 years and the competitor is quite new comparatively. So when it comes to overall margin manufacturers hardly have any say or control and they have to work within all these forces and limitations, while trying their own efforts in all directions to reduce costs and to be within the budgeted costs.

Innovation

This is another very sensitive area, where most of the manufacturers are not in position to have command and control. Because of low margins and many other reasons known to all, the expenditure on Research and Development field is low. Most companies cannot afford any allocation of funds due to financial crisis. We have enough talent in our country, but we cannot attract them with our standard pay packets, when compared with offers by others. Technology and technical expertise on any product is available in any country at almost negligible price, but we are not in position to buy it, when we need it most.

Some companies are so contented that they do not feel any necessity of introduction of new products in the markets. As regards the consumer and consumer durable products it is very essential since customers have become very choosy. In case of engineering products and own designed products companies should try and introduce newer features which would be user friendly and thus make the life of the users more comfortable. Entire new design at every year or two may not be possible, as you notice. Mere different range of products, with certain variation in some features, is being offered by the latest passenger car producers in our country.

Some other companies spend huge amounts on this field, but cannot keep pace with the world around and ultimately loose the battle. It is the time factor that also needs to be taken into consideration with a predetermined target date and also keeping a close eye on the competitors' movement in this direction. It was published in a business magazine that 'Sony'—the leading Japanese producer in electronic and household goods—a name known for the home and electronic products in India, launched around 379 products in a period between 1996 98.

Leadership

This personnel quality refers to the ability of the persons who are leading the organisations. In the first instance let us discuss about the ability of the top executives, who are heading the Indian companies today. This area enlists qualities like their vision about the future of the products manufactured by the company. Then their personal attributes like educational qualifications, foresight, decision-making ability, capacity of understand and manage financial matters, capacity of handling manpower, leading the team of persons with own examples, up to date knowledge on the market conditions and staying competitive and so on.

Top management leaders need to know about strategic planning, information technology, and human behaviour. For them the challenge is that the investment and risk are increasing constantly. More investment is necessary in technology upgradation, plant and machinery, brand building exercises, and building human resources. These areas call for more strategic decision-making ability and less of tactical operational knowledge. During the earlier license - permit system in our country, most of the talent and its energy was consumed on short-term operational leadership. Now the leaders have to take long-term decisions with a bit of risk and they need to have own source of confidence.

Another major challenge on leadership—whether it is of the organisations or the unions, is that the expectations of the employees are increasing at all the times. More compensation is one part but better career prospects is another, which is often taken as an incentives by the employees, specially the newer generation. They also expect them to be the decision-making process and given certain authority to deal with the situations directly.

The top industry leaders are always under the pressure of innovation, substitution of products. Thus their companies must always be more consistent about delivery, product mix, quality, safety of their products. Leaders must also be keen on social problems of poverty, jobs, quality of work life of the employees. Leaders should also operate reward and punishment system within their organisations so that the system clearly sends a message that short cuts are not permitted and only committed work behaviour is counted and rewarded.

Some senior and top executives posts in some companies are occupied by the persons retired from some other organisations. Their physical and mental state sometimes proves to be out of tune to understand the changes taking place around them and thus the whole organisation fails to cope with the market demands made by their customers from time to time. Same may be case with other seniors employed by the company who keep working with the help of same old tools and techniques.

Another area about the leadership points out the ability of persons at the helm of affairs of organisations working for workmen. The parameters enlisted above are equally applicable to these elected members also. Very few leaders are seen with ability to understand the changes and the speed at which these changes are happening around. One special quality is necessary and thus needs to be mentioned here, that the elected members must be 'people oriented'.

Elected leaders must keep themselves always with the sole objective of service to the people, and not the personal gains. Over the years, these leaders have found an easy access to the political field through these activities, where personal gains is the only motive. Our history also supports this fact and we have had many a leaders of workmen taking up important political positions later on in their career.

In the initial stages it may be advisable to look into the smaller problems of the workmen, but they must know that this is not their main area to work upon.

Some elected leaders follow a tact of drawing attention of workmen to minor issues and purposely divert them from some important ones. They keep workmen engaged with some fear about certain unworthy decisions by the top management and take a position of a soldier who is protecting them. Their main task would be to take people into confidence, provide them with adequate information on all matters and develop a level of confidence in their minds about him and about their company's management. As discussed under the topic of mutual trust in the earlier discussions, both of them have to work together and for many years to come, this feeling of faith and confidence is very essential for the healthy atmosphere within an organisation.

People oriented approach also calls for some more efforts on his part to take actions against the real care and welfare measures for the workmen, may be some of those related to their future and not of immediate needs. To practice this approach, one needs to put in extra efforts in learning new things, continuously guiding others with his experience and nurturing some basic values developed over the years by him in shaping his career and this must be seen clearly through his actions, not through his loud and spicy speaking.

I have come across some learned elected members who are armed with sufficient knowledge on preparation and reading of annual balance sheets of the companies where they are working. This knowledge certainly helps them while dealing with workmen and also with members of management team. This is what now needs to be told to all of them while dealing with workmen and also with members of management team. This is what now needs to be told to all of them and to officers dealing with the subject of industrial relations in industry, if they have to be successful in their career.

Various Approaches to Industrial Relations

The Oxford Approach

This approach has had a great deal of influence on the industrial relations thinking in U.K. According to this the industrial relations system is a study of institutions of job regulations and the stress is on the procedural rules. It is considered that every business enterprise as a social system of production and distribution, has a structured pattern of relationships. The 'institution of job regulation' is categorised here as having internal and external components. Internal part consists of code of work rules, wage structure, internal procedure for joint consultation and grievance handling procedure.

According to this approach Trade Union is an external organisaiton and thus excludes collective agreements from the spheres of internal regulations. According to it collective bargaining is central to the industrial relations system. This approach can be criticised on the ground that it is too narrow and does not provide comprehensive framework for analysing industrial relations problems. It over emphasises the significance of the political process of collective bargaining, thus giving more importance to institutional and power factors. It does not give importance to the factors like technology, market, status of the parts and their values systems.

This approach stresses the process of rule making through collective bargaining. This therefore was welcome by not only the public administration but by some of the younger scholars in industrial relations.

Industrial Sociology Approach

Though the earlier approach had sufficient level of acceptance in U.K. one industrial sociologist, G. Margerison, held the view that the, "basis of industrial relations is the 'nature and development of the conflict itself". He argued that conflict is the basic concept and as such it should form the basis of the study in this field.

According to this thought there are two levels of industrial relations. One level exists within the plant or works, where situational factors like job contents, work, task, technology and interaction factors produce various types of conflicts like structural type, human relation type etc. These conflicts can be sorted out by collective bargaining, structural analysis of the socio-technical systems and management, *i.e.* employer – employee, analysis.

The second level exists outside the organisation and concerns with all those conflicts not resolved within the plant. This approach rejects the importance to rules determination, but suggests that such conflicts can also be resolved.

Action Theory Approach

As the name suggests, all the four parts work within a group and within a framework. The action theory approach takes the collective industrial workforce as its target group; and bargaining negotiations.

Since this is action oriented approach, and always aimed at resolving some conflicts, there cannot be an uniform theory, because it changes from the nature of the conflicts from time to time.

The Marxist Approach

The class conflict analysis of industrial relations has its roots in marxist social thinking, which is basically a method of social enquiry into the power relationships existed within any society. Marxist approach is oriented towards the historical development of the power relationships between capital and labour. This is mainly the struggle between these two classes to consolidate and strengthen their own positions with the sole objective of exerting greater influence on each other.

Industrial relations, according to marxist, are in the first place market relations but it is not explained further. According to me it could be understood in two different meanings of market relations as "from where the business comes to the company (customers)", and "the place where sufficient workmen are available for jobs (employment)", without these two no company can work.

This approach therefore equates the industrial relations with power struggle. The price table for labour is determined by the capitalists with the ownership of the enterprise. Efforts are always directed to purchase the labour at the lowest possible price in order to maximise their profits. The lower the price paid to labour, it would increase the profits. This analysis as seen, is not a comprehensive one. The application of this theory as it relates to industrial relations derives indirectly from scholars working on marks in the early parts of last century.

Pluralism is a major theory in workmen—management relations which is powerly acknowledged allover. According to many a sociologist "social environment is an important factor in industrial conflicts". This isolated masses are more prone to strikes. When industrial jobs become more pleasant and employees get more integrated into the wider and larger society, strike shall be less in number and also the frequency. This is proved by data available which shows the decline in number of strikes allover in spite of increase in the memberships of unions.

These theories were evolved in mid sixties, when England witnessed increase in industrial conflicts. According to Flanders, a British scholar, " conflict is inherent in the industrial system". He insisted on development of formal system of collective bargaining as method for resolving any conflict.

There is another thought which distinguishes between two distinct aspects of relationship between the workmen and the management. The first is the market relationship which concerns with the terms and conditions of hiring the workmen. This relationship is essentially economic in character and based on the contracts executed between both the parties.

The second aspect of relationship relates to the management's dealing with workmen, the nature of its interaction, negotiations between the union and the management, distribution of power in the organisational structure and the participation of the elected members of the union in the decision-making process.

The Human Relations Approach

In the words of Keith Davies, human relations are "the interaction of people into a work situation that motivates them to work together productively, co-operatively and with economic, psychological and social satisfactions". According to him the goals of human relations are :

- To get people to produce.
- To co-operate through mutuality of interests.
- To gain satisfaction from their relationships.

The human relations school founded by Elton Mayo and later propagated by many offers a coherent view of the nature of industrial conflict and harmony. The human relations approach highlights certain policies and techniques to improve employee morale, efficiency and job satisfaction. It also encourages the small work groups to exercise considerable control over its environment and in the process assist to eliminate a major situations in labour-management relations.

This approach was criticised on the grounds that it encourage more dependency on the part of workmen on their employers, while discouraging individual development, and ignored the importance of technology and culture in the industry. If a balanced view is taken, it must be admitted that this approach has thrown open a lot of light on certain aspects of better communication. Management development, acceptance of workplace as social system, group dynamics, participation in management etc.

As regards the dependency is concerned, most of the industries have a system of payment of advances against the salaries and wages of the workmen, somewhere around middle of the month or as per the needs. The workman has to approach with his application to the personnel or welfare department, obtain the approval and he gets the amount, with or sometimes even without a genuine reason. This advance is a short-term loan without interest or at a low rate of interest, just a gesture of helping a workman. This loan is recovered from the monthly salary on an affordable instalment spread over a period corresponding to the amount to the recovered.

Salary advances have become over the years, a right exerted by the representatives of the workmen and often a clause regarding it, is present in the agreements. Now this advance is looked as "a no-interest amount easily available from the employer without much inquiry and trouble, for investment somewhere else", as such why not to ask for it very frequently and almost everyone in the organisation demands it. The day there is a circular or a notice regarding any revision on this matter, there is a conflict and representatives throng the office of the personnel officer for a protest.

In a real sense this practice should be looked as "means of keeping workmen under debt all the time" employed by the management and as such it should be discouraged by the representatives of the workmen, rather than fighting for it with the management, because once workmen get into habit of having extra money in the hands, they get habitual of it and expect the same, even when the loan is fully repaid, they would apply for a fresh one. This is a vicious circle and it is very difficult for any one to come out of it.

Similar is the case when some companies offer goods through the co-operative societies on credit to their workmen and the payments are recovered from their wages, thus making the workmen all the time dependable on the management for all his needs. Management should therefore design some policy in consultation with the representatives regarding this practice and implement it in a more practical way without sacrificing the interests of both the parties.

Dr. Udey Parekh and T.V. Rao have developed human relations concept in 1974 and practiced it at reputed companies and the same is now widely accepted by the industry since 1980. Their concepts are more concerned on nature of human beings as free creatures with basic inherent urges for self fulfilment and growth potentials. Similarly learned and expert Ravi Mathai, second director of IIM, Ahmedabad recommends the organisational structure to be such "where enough freedom would be for human competencies to develop, creating a culture, where people could work on their own, take risks and have their own evaluation mechanisms", is practiced for a long-term growth of the organisations.

There can be two approaches for solving the disputes and conflicts, considering the human relations as principle in dealing with the cases. The two approaches are : Preventive Approach considers human relations and it is based upon the principle that " prevention is better than cure". According to this approach the problems are objectively viewed and discussed with employees concerned, whether it is a case of indiscipline or disorderly behaviour.

While using this approach certain techniques like motivation, communication, inter personal relations practices, and counselling are often used by the seniors or superiors of the employee, or jointly by him with personnel from HR departments. Opportunity and guidance is provided to the employee to overcome the problems. Though it is a time consuming process, it is much sound and perfect, where by many of the conflicts in industries can be prevented. During the process two important exercises are carried out : Analysis and Counselling. During the stage of analysis, collection of facts and data is given utmost importance to avoid any misunderstanding and recording of false data which can lead to wrong interpretation. Such a data is verified from own sources to judge whether the incident is out of situation or due to human behaviour. This is a very important stage to fix up the focus of attention. Counselling is a specialised work and should be handled in a professional manner, because it involves all those above steps and three to four more aspects of human side, namely understanding the person, situation, application of psychology, use of sympathetic view of necessary, updating the person with facts and consequences, and extend assistance by way of suitable training and guidance.

Corrective Approach, as the name suggests, applied after the incident has occurred. Disciplinary procedures are initiated, without any efforts/steps towards understanding the human or situation behind such occurrence. Thus motivation and counselling etc. is absent here.

The Gandhian Approach

Mahatma Gandhi can be called as one of the greatest labour leaders of modern India. His approach to labour problems was completely newly and refreshingly human. He held definite views about fixation and regulation of wages, organisation and functions of trade unions, necessity and desirability of collective bargaining, use and abuse of strikes, labour in -discipline, workmen participation in management, conditions of work and living, duties of workmen etc. Many of his ideas were implemented then by the Ahmedabad Textile Labour Association, a unique and successful experiment in Gandhian trade unionism.

Gandhiji had great faith in the goodness of human beings and he believed that many of the evils of the modern world have been created by the wrong systems and not by wrong individuals. He insisted on recognising each individual worker as human being first. He believed in non-violent communism with some laid down conditions for a successful strike. Some of those conditions were :

- The cause of the strike must be just and there should be no strike without a justified grievance.
- There should be no violence.
- Non strikers should never be molested.
- Strikes should be used as last weapon, only when all peaceful and constitutional methods of negotiations, conciliation and arbitration get exhausted.

His concept of trusteeship is a significant contribution in the sphere of industrial relations. According to him employers should not take themselves as the owners of the mills and factories, though they may be in the legal terms, instead they should act as the trustees or co-owners of the units. He also appealed to the workmen to behave as trustees and not to treat the mills and machinery owned by the employers as means of exploitation. Workmen should treat the mills and factories as their own assets and protect those, and put to the best use. This theory of trusteeship is based on the view that "all forms of property and human achievements are gifts of nature, and as such all property belongs to the society and not to any individual".

Thus this trusteeship approach is totally different from the traditionally thought labour relations system. It is aimed at achieving economic equality and material advancement of the workmen. He put greater importance to change in attitudes of employers and insisted upon them to treat the workmen as co-partners in a joint venture. He also emphasised through his continuous writing on this subject, that workmen should be regarded as equal with the other shareholders and therefore they have equal right to know the commercial transactions and financial details on the working of the mills and factories. While pleading to the management, he expectecd them to share the benefits of higher productivity with the workmen, and initiate continuous efforts on job enrichment of them.

According to Gandhiji, workers refused to be ignored while at work. If his work and talents are not taken a note of and if his contributions to the industry are not measured periodically, he shall not give his best nor put in extra efforts to contribute more for the successful completion of his job and duties. Workmen have enough potential of creativity and improvement in all systems. As we often mention in our sessions on quality improvement and implementation of Total Quality Management workshops, this potential is rarely utilised by the present day management systems in our country.

In this chapter we shall discuss briefly few laws related to industrial discipline and misconduct by an employee. In enquiry held by the management against any of its employees for certain act of alleged misconduct is called "domestic enquiry" or departmental enquiry. Now under the existing judicial decisions, management cannot punish its employee for an act of misconduct unless reasonable opportunity is given to him to defend it, and unless it is proved. Any enquiry is concerned with determining whether charges leveled against him can be established or not. The enquiry also serves the purpose to determine nature of punishment upon the guilty workman. Domestic enquiry is subject to the principles of natural justice and procedure laid down by the court.

Disciplinary Action

Model standing orders under the Industrial Employment [Standing Orders] Act, 1946 provide for disciplinary action for misconduct. The Act gives an illustrative list of acts omissions which can be regarded as misconduct. All establishments whether they have their own Certified Standing orders or they follow Model Standing orders [as per Act] are required to follow the standard procedure for awarding a punishment against such a misconduct.

In a disciplinary action the charge sheet is very important, which is issued to an employee stating the charges. This is based upon the principles of natural justice which states that "the guilty person should know about his guilt so that he is able to put forward his say in reply to the charges. He should be given an opportunity to place his explanation before his seniors or the officer to defend himself". Such a written explanation can, once read by officials, and if found with satisfactory substance, avoid enquiry and other proceedings. Even charge sheet, when framed against a person, is not an accusation, because he still has a right to defend the charges with all proofs and witnesses.

Upon completion of detailed enquiry, the enquiry officer submits a report on all findings of the case but without mention of or recommendation of any punishment. The higher managers at plant level think on this report and if found him guilty, award the right kind of punishment from the followings :

(1) warning

(2) fine

(3) stoppage of annual increments

(4) demotion

(5) suspension

(6) discharge or dismissal.

The first five are minor punishments but the last one is major one. Award of punishment should be according to standing orders, however management has discretion to award any appropriate one, subject to gravity and nature of the offence, but is should not be unduly excessive. According to ordinary law that, "a person having power of employment can terminate the services", but the right to exercise this major punishment should also be used carefully.

Natural Justice

The concept of natural justice has different meanings in different contexts. It is humanising principle to invest law with fairness and secure justice. There is a set of rules laid down by courts for minimum protection of rights of an induvidual against any arbitrary procedure or decision arrived at. It is application of fair play, impartiality and natural sense of "what is right and what is wrong" in any given context. As said earlier, it is humanising concept and hence its principles apply differently in different situations.

The concept of natural justice has undergone a great changes in these days. Earlier it had only two thoughts included, like a person cannot act as a judge if he is party to the dispute, and hears the other side, other party. Now third thought is included that, enquiry must be held in good faith, without bias, not arbitrarily or unreasonably. The party is entitled to know the reason for decision, not just the decision, is also the part of the natural justice.

The principles of natural justice in holding an enquiry against an employee are, the charge sheeted person should be given a notice of a proposed enquiry to be held, no one should be condemned behind his back, or in his absence, the charges should be made known to him, he should be given reasonable opportunity to defend himself, all documents and evidences against the charges should be recorded in presence of the employee and all material should be seen by him with an opportunity to explain if he wishes, he should have an opportunity to cross-examine the witnesses brought against him, so also bring his own evidence and witnesses. The enquiry officer can obtain information and materials from all sources and through all channels, but it is obligatory on him by the law, that he should show all these to the person against whom the same is going to be used and also give an opportunity to him to explain on those. If the departmental proceedings and criminal proceedings if any, against the same person arise out of the same set of facts and circumstances, departmental enquiry should be stayed till proceedings are over before the trial court.

The elementary principle of natural justice is that parties should be given opportunity, a reasonable one, to defend their rights before the tribunal or the labour court. This opportunity includes giving sufficient time, suitable date so that they can prepare their case and make arrangements for representations. Domestic enquiry is claimed to be a managerial function. A person from the organisation plays a role of a judge. It is held in his department or in his office. The enquiry officer combines the judge and the prosecutor both into one. Generally it is found that there are legally trained minds work for the employer, but the employee is deprived of the same. He should also be given the same assistance, because justice given should be seen by all.

The Industrial Employment [Standing Orders] Act, 1946

Origin

Before studying the acts regarding working conditions and terms of service, it would worth while to know about the English Factory Acts between 1833 to 1864. Prior to the period of 1833 young persons and child were working all night, all day or both sometimes. A normal working day for modern industry only started from the Factory Act, 1833, made applicable to cotton, wool, flax, silk factories.

The Act of 1833 declared the ordinary factory working day from 5.30 a.m. to 8.30 p.m.—15 hours. a day. It was lawful to employ young persons between the age of 13 to 18 years, at any time of the day, provided individual person works for not more than 12 hrs. in any one day. The 6th sec. Of the Act provided for one and half hour for meals to everyone.

Children below the age of 9 yrs. Werer not permitted for employment. Working hours for children between 9 and 13 were restricted to 8 Hrs. a day. Thus two sets of children: one from 5.30 a.m. to 1.30 p.m. and the other from 1.30 p.m. to 8.30 p.m. were put to work. The age limit for employment of children with amendments, was:

1st March, 1834 age under 11 yrs.

1st March, 1835 age under 12 yrs.

1st March, 1836 age under 13 yrs.

and also the working day was reduced to 8 Hrs. per day.

But soon capital began a noisy agitation which went on for several yrs. Mainly on the age of those employed under the name of children were limited to 8 hours work and subject to a certain amount of compulsory education. The Act remained unaltered until 1844. The Act of 1833, left the options with the Lords of the factories and reports of the factory inspectors stated that it was impossible to monitor the actual working hours since, "Young persons, children begin, break off, resume and end at any moment, they (lords) liked. Similarly they assigned different persons, different times for meals and children were constantly re-harnessed at changing work stations." Thus it was difficult to enforce the legally determined "work time" and "meals times". This work system was explained to the Home Secretary in 1844.

During September, 1844 additional Act came into force. This gave protection to a new category of workers *i.e.* women over 18 years of age; with same terms as young persons with 12 years work per day. The working time was reduced to 6.5 hours for children, with specific mention that, no child or young person shall be employed for more that five hours before 1.0 p.m. without any interval for meal time for minimum 30 minutes.

A further amendment titled under The New Factory Act, which came into effect in May, 1848 brought the limitations on working day to 10 hours a day, but the owners also reduced the pay accordingly upto fifty per cent. The conditions in India were also similar to this. We find all these changes were brought about and laws were developed for modern production system, with strong and continued struggle between the classes. Just like a battle human beings are having with life for their progress, development and survival.

History

There was no uniform practice regarding the conditions of service of workmen until this. The Industrial Employment (standing orders) Act, 1946, was brought into force. The absence of standing orders, defining clearly the rights and obligations of the employer and the workmen were found to be major reasons for industrial relation problems between both of them. The Bombay Industrial Disputes Act, 1938 for the first time provided for the statutory standing orders. The Labour Investigation Committee, 1944-46 observed that an industrial workman has the right to know the terms and conditions under which he is employed and the rules of discipline he is expected to follow. This was a result of the fact that, this matter was earlier brought before the fifth Labour Conference in 1943, 44 and 45. Thus the Act was passed on 23rd April, 1946 but it came force w.e.f. 1st April, 1947.

This Act was amended in May, 1982 for sec. 10-A which provided for the payment of subsistence allowance by the employer to the employee, during suspension pending enquiry at the rate of fifty per cent of the wages for the first 90 days and seventy five per cent for the remaining period. The objective of this Act was that terms and conditions of service should be defined by the employees and made known to the workmen. The other objectives were to bring uniformity in terms and conditions of employment, to foster harmonious relations between them and to reduce industrial conflicts.

Scope

This Act extends its scope to the whole of India. It is applicable to all industrial establishments, employing 100 workmen or were employed during last twelve months. Once it becomes applicable to any establishment, even when the number of employees is decreased, it continues there. In 1961, the Act was amended for the condition of minimum number of employees to less than 100, and empowered to state Governments to act accordingly by giving a notice of two months to such establishments. In response to this, the Government of Maharashtra applied all provisions of the Act from 15th August, 1982 to any establishment where 50 or more employees were employed on any day of the preceding twelve months. The Government has the powers to exempt any establishment or classes of establishments from any or all the provisions of the Act. The Act covers all industrial establishments, including public sector enterprises, except where the provisions of The Bombay Industrial Relations Act, 1946 are applicable.

The Act has 15 sections in all and a schedule. It is applicable, as said earlier, to all workmen employed in any industrial establishment, performing any skilled or unskilled, manual, supervisory, technical or clerical type of work, jobs. Apprentices undergoing training under the Apprenticeship Act, 1961 are also covered under this Act.

Persons employed in managerial or administrative capacities, and those working in supervisory capacity with salary more than Rs. 1600 p.m. are not covered under this Act while entertaining any industrial dispute.

Standing orders, certified by the authorities and in practice in any industrial establishment shall and can undergo any change, after a period of six months from the date of last modification was brought in force, with the agreement between the employer and the workmen. The idea of allowing this period of six months, is to see that any modification works properly or whether it creates any difficulty or problems while working to any group of employees or the employer. However this period limit is also flexibly modified by the agreement between the two parties. Whenever such modifications are proposed, one copy of such agreement between the two parties, duly certified, should be submitted to the Certifying Officer along with the application for modification.

The standing orders of an industrial establishment which have been duly certified under the Act then become the part of the statutory terms and conditions of service between the employer and his employees and govern all the relations between them as regards all matters covered by the standing orders. Thus no oral evidence of effect of additions or alterations varying these terms and conditions shall be admitted in any court. An employer who fails to submit a draft of modification, in other than a specified form under sec. 10 is punishable with fine of suitable amount. Similarly any employer who acts in contradiction to the certified standing orders is also punishable with a suitable fine.

If any question arises as to the application or interpretation of standing orders certified under the Act, the employer or workmen or trade union or other representing body of the workmen can refer the question to any one of the Labour Court constituted under the Industrial Disputes Act, 1947. The Labour Court then shall, after giving the parties an opportunity of being heard, decides the question. The functions of the Labour Court under the Act are limited only to the decision of the question as to the application or interpretation of the standing orders which are referred to it. It does not have powers to grant relief or violations of the rights and obligations created under these standing orders.

The law laid down till recently has been that the standing orders of a company describe certain acts but the same cannot be exhaustive of all the categories of misconduct which a workman may commit. In a given context, an act [a misconduct] may not fall under the specific acts of misconduct as listed in the standing orders, but which can still be a misconduct in the substantial facts of the case. If there is a clause in the standing orders treating absence or extension of leave as misconduct, the management is entitled to proceed against the workman. Similarly on the part of workmen on probation period, there can be provisions regarding the duration and its extension.

The Bombay Industrial Relations Act, 1946

The government of Bombay enacted the Bombay Industrial Disputes Act, 1938 which came into force with effect from 1st June, 1939. Subsequently the Bombay Industrial Relations Act, 1947 was brought in and was enforced in 1947, replacing the Act of 1938. This Act is based on three Gandhian principles, namely negotiation, conciliation and arbitration. The main objectives of this Act are :

Objectives

- To provide machinery for settlement of disputes by adjudication or arbitration on considerations of justice, equity and good conscience.
- To promote collective bargaining.
- To regulate relations between employers and the employees for harmonious relations between them.

The Act extends to the states of Maharashtra and Gujarat and is applicable only to certain industries like textile processing – cotton, silk, hosiery, woollen – sugar, co-operative banking generation and supply of energy and transport [BEST undertaking]. The term 'employee' means under this Act, any person employed to do a skilled or unskillled work for hire or reward in any industry, including persons engaged by a contractor but not the persons in the managerial, administrative, supervisory or technical capacity drawing basic pay exceeding Rs. 1000 p.m.

Special Feature

A peculiar feature of the Act is that in addition to the registration of a union as a Representative Union, it recognises another class of union as Approved Union. This is dealt with in chapt. 4 of the Act. The Registrar can enter the name of the union on the approved list if the union makes an application in that regard and if the rules provide for it. The Registrar may not enter the union in the approved list if he is satisfied that it is not in the bona fide interest of its members. If two or more unions fulfilling the conditions necessary for being entered in the approved list, apply in respect of the same industry in any local area, in the same calendar month, the union having the largest membership of employees in that industry, in the calendar month immediately preceding month in which it applied, shall be entered in the approved list.

If any union disapproved earlier, but claims larger membership in that industry after a period of two years since, inclusion of other union in the approved list, applies to the Registrar for its inclusion, then the Registrar may, after holding enquiry, enter its name in the approved list. In such an event, the aggrieved union, within 30 days from the date of the order, may appeal against such order to the Industrial Court.

The approved union has certain rights regarding collection of sums from its members, put up notices on the board on the premises of the undertaking, to hold discussions on the premises with the concerned employees, to inspect any place of working in case of settlement of dispute, and to appear before the Labour Court or Industrial Court with necessary legal aid at the cost of the State Government. In such court proceedings, Association of employers is also entitled to represent any employer.

Changes in Standing Orders

Regarding Standing Orders, the Act has made elaborate provisions for settlement. Before settling these orders or alterations, views of the representative union or in the absence of the representative union, views of the elected representative are considered. Until standing orders under the provisions of this Act come into operation in an undertaking, the Model Standing Orders are applicable. After settlement of standing orders, they remain in operation for at least one year, thereafter any of the parties can apply for change in it.

Any employee or a representative union desiring a change in respect of any order passed by the employer under, standing orders or any industrial matter arising out of the application or the interpretation of standing orders, has to approach the employer with a request for a change, and if no agreement has been arrived at in respect of such a change, can make an application to the Labour Court or the Industrial Court, as the case may be. The employer cannot make any change in the standing orders settled as per the provisions of this Act, without following the procedure. Similarly failure to carry out the terms of settlement, registered agreement, effective order or a decision of Labour Court or the Industrial Court, affecting industrial matters is deemed to be an illegal change.

Generally some minor or major matter is sufficient for industrial and rest somewhere in any industry, which results in poor industrial relations between the two parties. The union sometimes resort to illegal stoppage of work, or illegal strikes and then considering the safety of the plan and buildings, the management initiates the closure, which sometimes legal or illegal. The Act has clear definitions and elaboration on legality of such matters and the conditions under which these are treated as illegal.

Joint Committees

According to the provisions pertaining to formation of joint committees, the same can be constituted for an undertaking or occupation with the concern of the employer and the registered union for the industry. But such a committee is normally not constituted where there is no representative union. The joint committee consists of an equal number of members from both, the employer and the union. These members try to resolve the matters concerning with cleanliness, hygiene, canteen, welfare etc. The decisions of the Joint Committee carry a great weight, but are not final. Similarly it is not their duty to take decisions on important matters such as alterations of conditions of service.

CHAPTER

2

Trade Union

Introduction—Trade Union

A trade union is a complex, dynamic, social institution, because it has economic, social, political and psychological aspects. It is also flexible in nature, so that it can change with the changes in the environment. The trade unions are formed to protect and improve economic, social, political and vocational interests of the workers and also to strengthen the bargaining power of its members.

Definitions

The term Trade Union has been defined by various authorities as follows:

(*i*) "Trade Union is the continuous long period worker's organization which is meant for attainment of specific objectives to protect the interests of its members and for the improvement of labour relations."

– Dale Yoder

(*ii*) "A Trade Union is an association of employees designed primarily to maintain or improve the conditions of employment of its members".

– Laster

(*iii*) "A Trade Union is a continuous association of wage earners for the purpose of maintaining or improving the conditions of their working force".

– Webb

(*iv*) "A Trade Union is the worker's organization which is established by their collective activities to the welfare of the members in social, economic and political interests and to keep them secured and for improvement in it". – *Edwin B. Flippo*

(*v*) "A Trade Union means an association of workers in one or more occupations, an association carried on mainly for the purpose of protecting and advancing the member's economic interests in connection with their daily work". – *G.D.H.Cole*

(*vi*) "Trade Union is a monopolistic competition of wage earners who stand to the employer's in a relation of dependence for the sale of their labour and even for its production and that the general purpose of the association is in view of that dependence to strengthen their power to bargain with the employers".

– *Cunningham*

(*vii*) "A Trade Union is such an organization which is created voluntarily on the basis of collective strength to secure the interests of the workers". – *V.V.Giri*

(*viii*) "A Trade Union is any combination, whether temporary or permanent, formed primarily for the purpose of regulating the relations between workmen and employers or between workers and workers, between employers and employers or for imposing restrictive conditions on the conduct of any trade or business and includes any federation of two or more trade unions".

(*ix*) "A Trade Union is a continuous and voluntary association of the salary or wage earners and engaged in whether industry or trade, formed for safeguarding the interests of its members, maintaining and improving their vocational interests, and securing better relations between them and their employers through collective bargaining". – *C.B.Memoria*

Main Features of Trade Union

Following are the basic characteristics of Trade Unions:

(*i*) The Trade Union is a voluntary and continuous organization of employees or employers or of independent workers.

(*ii*) The Trade Unions are generally permanent association of workers and they are not casual or temporary in nature.

(*iii*) The Trade Unions are dynamic social institutions; hence they can adjust themselves to the changes in the environment.

(*iv*) The basic objectives of the Trade Unions are to protect social, economic and vocational interests of their members and to contribute towards and socio-economic development of the country.

(*v*) The Trade Unions are able to meet the challenges generated by the changes in technology as well as changes in the environment.

(*vi*) The origin and growth of Trade Unions have been influenced by several ideologies.

(*vii*) The Trade Unions are the outcome of an individualistic society.

(*viii*) Trade Unions are formed by wage earners for undertaking collective action. The main object is to increase the bargaining power of the workers so as to negotiate with the employers very effectively.

(*ix*) A Trade Union works as a collective agent for its members for the purpose of negotiating for wages, working conditions, hours of work, terms and conditions of service, etc.

Objectives and Role of Trade Unions

We may summarise below the several functions undertaken by the Trade Unions as follows:

(*i*) To improve working and living conditions of the workers.

(*ii*) To secure fair wages for themselves.

(*iii*) To promote individual and collective welfare.

(*iv*) To safeguard security of tenure and improve conditions of service.

(*v*) To enlarge opportunities for promotion and training.

(*vi*) To provide educations, cultural and recreational facilities.

(*vii*) To promote identity of the interests of the workers with their industry.

(*viii*) To co-operate and facilitate technological progress by explaining the workers the problems and advantages of such progress.

(*ix*) To develop sense of responsibility towards industry and community amongst the members.

(*x*) To fulfil certain social responsibilities such as integration, influencing socio-economic policies of local community through active participation etc.

(*xi*) To acquire control of industry by workers.

(*xii*) To develop self-confidence and sincerity, honesty and discipline amongst the members.

(*xiii*) To promote morale of the workers.

(*xiv*) To promote national integration.

Functions of Trade Union

According to the Trade Union's Act – 1926, the main objective of the Trade Union is to protect and promote the interests of the workers and the conditions of their employment. To protect interests of the workers implies getting reasonable wages, improved working conditions, shorter working hours, greater security of the person and the job.

In order to achieve the above stated objectives, the Trade Unions undertake several functions. These functions may be classified as follows:

Intramural Functions

Those functions, which are internal or lie within the four walls of the factory are known as 'intramural functions'. These include improvement of activities like wages, sanitation, safety, continuity of employment, rest interval etc.these functions are described as Militant or Protective functions, because, in order to perform these functions, the workers have to adopt strikes, boycotts, gheraos and other measures when collective bargaining process is not successful.

Extramural Functions

These are the functions, which are external to the organization. These functions are also known as external or positive functions that are carried out to help the members in times of need. These include the provision of education, recreational, housing etc. facilities by the Unions. The Unions raise funds by way of collecting subscriptions from their members, which are utilized for providing necessary facilities to the member workers. These functions are considered as important because they promote the spirit of co-operation and self-sacrifice for the welfare of the other members, and to serve common interests.

Political Functions

The past history of Indian Trade Unions indicates that political leaders like Tilak, Gandhi served as the Trade Union leaders. Even today, the leadership is provided by the political leaders. The intention was to realize socio-economic objectives of the unions through legislative and administrative measures. The Unions are authorized to raise funds for political purposes such as expenditure on election of labour representatives, holding political meeting, etc. but the impact of the external political leadership was adverse for healthy development of Trade Unions in India. These political leaders used the Trade Unions as means to serve their political ends.

Social Functions

These functions include several social service activities undertaken by the Union for discharging their social responsibilities like—providing educational facilities, arranging sports competitions etc.

Ancilliary Functions

In addition, the Trade Unions carry out several ancilliary functions as follows:

(*i*) Welfare Facilities: The Unions may provide welfare facilities like—establishing co-operative housing societies, co-operative credit society, organizing training programmes, co-operative canteens and stores etc.

(*ii*) Educations Programmes: The Trade Unions also provide educational facilities for its members and their family members.

(*iii*) Communication: Trade Unions also communicate to their members various activities, programmes etc. undertaken through arranging meetings and publications of house magazines, news letters etc.

(*iv*) Research Activities: Unions may systematically collect relevant data and analyze it in order to generate information to be used for various purposes such as for collective bargaining, for court cases and for preparing notes for Union Officials. They may collect and analyze aggregate data for industries, economy or some sectors of the economy.

Advantages of Trade Unions

Trade Unions as dynamic and important social institutions generate several advantages not only to the labour but also to the employers and even the society at large. These advantages may be stated as follows:

Advantages to Labour

(*i*) Trade Unions promote unity and solidarity and co-operation among workers.

(*ii*) Trade Unions may contribute significantly towards promoting overall development of the workers.

(*iii*) Trade Unions, by way of providing healthy working conditions help in increasing production, productivity and efficiency of the workers.

(*iv*) Trade Unions, through creating equal counterveiling powers promotes collective bargaining between the parties with equal strength.

(*v*) Trade Unions are useful in avoiding exploitation of the workers.

(*vi*) Strong and healthy Trade Union provides opportunities for the workers to participate in the process of management of the organization.

(*vii*) Trade Unions also help their members to improve their economic and social status and enjoy satisfactory life.

(*viii*) Unions also help in maintaining the wages at the uniform level in terms of actual economic value.

Advantages to the Employers

Trade Unions help in reducing industrial conflicts, and even if they arise, then Unions help to solve them effectively.

Union promotes co-operation and team spirit among the workers which is essential for promoting and maintaining industrial peace.

Trade Unions, by encouraging the members to participate in the human developmental activities like training, education, entertainment etc. facilities enables the organization to have a large stock of trained, qualified and effective labour force.

Advantages to the Society and Nation

Labour Unions represent the views of working class regarding the problems faced by the workers, their ideas and feeling about social issues. This enables the society to know the labour problems and public opinion may compel the Government to enact legislation to protect and promote interests of the working class. It may enable the Government to work out labour policies and plan for the optimum utilization and development of human resources in the country. We may conclude that the Trade Unions not only promote efficiency and productivity of the workers, but also promotes co-operation among the members and train them to become responsible citizens of the nation, eager to contribute towards economic development of the country. The union can create suitable atmosphere for establishing industrial democracy in the country.

Various Theories of Trade Unions

There are several theories regarding the concept, evolution and practice of trade unionism. These theories may be summarized as follows:

Moral and Ethical Theories

During 19th century Christian Socialists argued that trade unions were formed to promote ethical and moral values in the society. It is the accumulation of wealth, which is responsible for evils it the society. Maurice and Kingley insisted upon the principle of brotherhood of man and mutual obligations. The development of culture gave rise to an opposition to poverty and injustices. It's the moral responsibility of the Trade Union to mobilize the resources of the weaker members of the population and to attain full realization of their energies. It was out of the compassion for the suffering's of the poor people in the society that led to the demand for justice, which resulted into the development of unionism. These theories are based on idealistic view of the situation where glaring inequalities and interpersonal competition prevails. Under such conditions it is the use of power, which enables the weaker section of the society to secure justice. However these moral and Ethical theories have failed to consider the use of power by the trade unions to achieve justice.

Socio-Psychological Theory

Robert F. Hoxie argued that the development of trade unions takes place not only because of economic factor but socio-psychological factors are also responsible for them. His approach is known as "Pluralistic casual interpretation of trade unionism". According to him, unionism affects not only production but also the established rights, ethical standards, distribution, law and order and exercise of general power over social conditions and psychological conditions of its member. The different types of unions emerge on account of the differences in group-psychology. He classified the unions on the basis of their structure and functional operations as follows:

(a) ***Business Unionism or Bread and Butter Unionism:*** Business unions are trade conscious than class-conscious and aims at achieving short-term economic goals like better wages, good working conditions rather than political and social demands. These unions are conservative as they accept the existing capitalistic organization and wage system and try to achieve their goals through collective bargaining and if it fails they adopt strikes as effective weapon.

(b) ***Friendly or Uplift Unionism:*** These unions are idealistic in nature and aim at improving moral, intellectual and social development of the member. It aims at implementing idealistic plans for social regeneration within the existing legal framework. Although they use collective bargaining technique still they depend more upon the weapon of strike. These unions are temperate and co-operative and are ready to compromise but they are observed to be very tough when they adopt direct action such as strike. They prefer to keep memberships limited to maintain better control and higher efficiency.

(c) ***Revolutionary Unionism:*** This type unions are very radical both in thought and action. They are class conscious and not trade-conscious. They are against private ownership of the means of production and the wage system. They prefer political and direct actions in the form of violence, general strikes etc. these unions are of two types.

(d) ***Socialistic Unions:*** Which aim at establishment of socialist system in place of capitalist system, prefer political actions and aim at establishing socialist state as an ultimate end of union activities. Collective bargaining may be used to improve working condition of the workers but emphasis in general is on direct or political action.

(e) ***Predatory Unionism:*** These are unions managed and controlled by gangsters. They do not have any ideology but are ready to adopt such methods, which could deliver goods immediately. They are not ready to pay attention towards ethicality on legality of their actions or decisions, and may adopt friendly or revolutionary methods.

According to Hoxie, there is one more type of unionism as Dependent Unionism. This type may take two forms depending upon whether such a union is supported by management to function in company unionism or by labour to work as label unionism.

Hoxie also observed that, although there are several types of trade unions, there is no guarantee that the existing union may be exactly of a particular type discussed above. Because the operation or functioning of the union defends upon relative strength of contending groups, factions within its membership and changes in economic conditions of the members. Hence unions may progress from one functional type to the other.

Thus Hoxie has adopted historical and positive approach and concludes that a solution for solving the conflicts between the employees and employers in fixation of socially recognized maxima and minima of rights and standards of behaviours which seems to be practically very difficult proposition.

Sociological Theory

Frank Tannenbaum argued that the emergence of trade unionism is the result of the workers reactions to the philosophy of individualism that prevailed during 19th and 20th centuries. Industrial Revolution destroyed the older economic order and left individual workers entirely dependent upon the capitalists. Thus the capitalist employers served as a catalytic agent making workers as a self-conscious group.

Tennenbaum argued that workers get engaged in an unconscious rebellion against the automation of industrial society. A sense of identity develops among men working at a common task and a trade union comes into existence.

According to him, rise of unionism is inherent in the growth of capitalism. It is not merely an economic organization but it is also a social and ethical institution as its ends are moral and not economic because it tries to re-establish the values where a man had formed dignity. By way of developing a strong organization, a union aims at achieving monopoly of the supply of labour to the trade or industry. It may prevent non-co-operative or non-union members from performing tasks covered by its jurisdiction. Once they establish their monopoly power, then they can dominate in wage bargain. These unions are able to drive out of business those firms, which cannot afford to pay the wages. The union has tended to strengthen the monopoly power to which it initially opposed. The workers created union to make their bargaining effective but now these unions become so powerful that they have reduced both worker members and the employers to a subordinate position.

According to him the quarrel between management and workers is in the nature of family quarrel as the two opposite parties are two sides of the same institution. As every activity of management affects the welfare of the workers, the unions, in order to protect interests of the workers steadily invade management prerogatives. So Tannenbaum predicts that this process will result into taking over of all the functions of the management by the unions. The process will accumulate their welfare funds and will purchase the corporations. But then the control of modern corporations by unions will create several problems. It will re-establish a society of status along with restrictions upon personal mobility and freedom of workers so that the worker will be tied to the union and also to the corporation that is under the control of union.

According to him the main feature of Trade Unionism is its lack of ideology and its concentration on short team end. It is unconscious rebellion against the automation of industrial society unionism has no solution because it is not a problem but it is a process inherent in industrial society. A trade union gives back to the worker his society and code of conduct by which he can live. In this sense Trade Unionism is counter revolutionary.

Scarcity Consciousness Theory

Selig Perlman on the basis of the study of trade unions in England, Germany, Russia and USA concluded that three factors are basic in any labour situation. These are: (1) The resistance power of capitalism determined by won historical developments; (2) The degree of dominance over the labour movement by the intellectual's mentality which regularly underestimates it; (3) The degree of maturity of a trade union-mentality.

Perlman argues that the unionism comes into existence because of scarcity consciousness of workers. When workers find that their wage income is hardly sufficient to meet their primary needs they cannot improve their economic position. Hence their scarcity consciousness tends to increase rapidly which gets reflected into job conscious unionism where a unionism controls job opportunity. The union prepares rules and regulations relating to overtime, promotion etc. that are binding to its member. Although the union does not replace the employer as the risk taker and the owner of business, it becomes the administrator of the scarce job opportunities.

Perlman argued that American Unionism has developed on account of scarcity consciousness and is evident in sharing the job opportunity rather than the communism of production and distribution. "Since the union expects its members to sacrifice for the group on a scale almost commensurate with the sacrifices which patriotism involves, it cannot be without its own respectable ideology".

Perlman also concluded that intellectuals are generally non-workers or outsiders and they try to impose their ideology on the labour movement. They believe that the economic conditions of the workers can only be improved by the acceptance of their ideology. Although these intellectuals differ significantly regarding causes and measures of the ills of society, they have common desire to use unions as weapons to bring about major social economic and political changes.

He believes that the American Federation of Labour (AFL) has been a successful organization in adjusting its organization and policies to the environment on the basis of the workers, recognizing the resistance power of American capitalism and avoiding the programmes of intellectuals. It has been confirmed by the stability of the membership and its capacity to face consequences of depressions. He has also stated that the labour movement has been a potent attack on the institution of private property. Trade unions, by using weapons like strikes, boycotts, working rules, securing government restrictions on employees, etc. try to restrict absolute right of the property workers find it difficult to organize themselves in the form of permanent union due to absence of class cohesiveness among them. They do not join the union on their own automatically and they are also not ready to make personal sacrifices to the union on their own automatically and they are also not ready to make personal sacrifices to maintain permanently active unions. It is the self-interest of the skilled workers the unions are formed and the workers were attracted to become member by attaining short-term economic needs and adopted overt means of preventing rebellion within their ranks.

Non-revolutionary Approach or Industrial Democracy Approach

Sydney and B. Webb argued that the separation of direction and execution of industrial operations were responsible for the development of trade unions. According to them, trade unions are the institutions for overcoming managerial dictatorship of conditions under which they have to work. Trade union is some voice in the determination of conditions under which they have to work. Trade union is not an instrument for the revolutionary overthrow of the capitalist order but it is a means of equalizing the bargaining power of labour and capital and thus encouraging the adoption of common rules, which are practical and humane.

Webbs argued that the purpose of the unions is not merely achieving economic benefits for the members but they aim at practical goals such as reconstruction of society by eliminating capitalists and to reduce the class of people who live merely by ownership of means of production.

According to Webbs the pressure put upon workers by unfavourable terms in market caused them to organize into unions to protect their interests. The chain or bargains linking together the manual worker, employee, the wholesale trader, the shopkeeper and the customer determined the conditions of employment. The pressure began with the customer and steadily increased with each link in the chain until it made the employers to produce most efficiently through optimum use of available resources so as to hold labour and other costs at minimum.

In order to improve economic status of the members, unions wanted that each firm pays a minimum rate and provide at least minimum working conditions regarding hours of work, sanitation, safety etc. Webs called them as "Common Rules".

The unions generally used the three methods to bring about continuous improvement in the Common Rules.

1. Initially they relied on mutual insurance through common subscription and unions financed programmes for the needy, aged and unemployed members.
2. The other method was to press for protective legislation especially during the 18th century, which regulated safety conditions in factories.
3. The third method is that of collective bargaining commonly adopted since 1924 of eliminate the need for individual action by the employers. So the trade unions have a permanent function to fulfil in the democratic state. Political democracy is not sufficient, as there is a need of having freedom of opportunity to use power that unions have to compel other to accept their terms. What is necessary is the establishment of "Industrial Democracy" where the workers are given good scope in managing the industry. The democratic administration of industry is the main function of trade unions. The employees and trade workers should work as equals.

General Approach to Trade Unionism

Dunlop and others observe that the worker protest is inherent in the process of industrialization. The workers protest because of stresses and strains generated by industrialisation. Organized form of protest is in the nature of labour union. The nature and role of such organization depends upon the industrialization process, industrializing elite, the specific culture and the environment of the country.

These authors emphasise that the traditional analysis of labour problem. Concentrates on the study of labour movement and unionism on the basis of the date relating to western developed countries mainly as a response to capitalism. In order to understand real nature and growth of unionism we should not take narrower approach covering western capitalist environment, but go for a wider field. So the author use the general term Labour Organization in place of Trade Union.

According to these authors the universal response of the labour force to industrialization is protest against it because it requires a basic change in relationship between man and his work and also between man and his cultural setting. The new recruit to the industrial labour force resents. The imposed discipline, which circumscribes his freedom. He has to deal with distasteful tasks and he is not sure that he will get adequate compensation to satisfy his needs and as a proper reward for his efforts. His feeling of insecurity continues for even under dynamic conditions surrounding him.

Kerr and his associates argue that there are five ideal types of the leadership of industrialization process as follows:

(i) ***Dynastic Elite Leadership:*** Under such a leadership the unions undertake social functions at the plant level and participate in practical activities challenging the employee. The workers join the unions in large number and having competing centralized federations. The leadership rests with intellectuals with political interests. Mostly the unions are class conscious and revolutionary.

(ii) ***Middle Class Elite Leadership:*** The unions under this type of leadership aim at regulating the management at local and industry level. They may undertake political activities, which do not challenge the employers. The workers themselves lead these Unions. They are reformists in their ideology.

(iii) ***Revolutionary Intellectual Elite Leadership:*** The unions under this type of leadership function as a main weapon in the hands of party to educate and lead workers and to promote production and political activities. There are few industrial unions affiliated to a centralized federation. The experienced party workers are the leaders of these unions. Ideologically the unions are followers of ruling elite.

(iv) ***Colonial Administrator Elite Leadership:*** Under it the unions function as a part of nationalist and independence movement. Their structure and organization differs widely, which are not developed. The leader is nationalist independent and intellectual having large follow up. Such unions ideologically are anti-colonial and fight for independence.

(v) ***Nationalist Elite Leadership:*** The Unions aim at achieving the objectives of economic development and protection of workers. There is a tendency towards industrial unions with one federation acceptable to the elite, national leaders and intellectuals provide leadership to such unions and the ideology of their union is nationalism.

Kerr concludes that, the type of labour organization that develops in a country is related to the type of industrializing elite. There are certain universals and the diversities that can be explained in terms of the strategies of industrializing elite's, cultures and environments. Labour protest in now showing tendency towards decline and it can even be controlled.

Marxian Theory of Trade Unionism

According to Marx trade unions are mainly the instruments of class struggle between Proletariat (workers) and bourgeois's (capitalists). Marx argued that as capitalism develops, the seeds of its destruction also develop simultaneously. Unequal distribution of income and wealth not only makes poor workers still poorer but also reduces their purchasing power, hence the effective demand declines and capitalists are not able to sale their output. So they reduce investment and production that give rise to trade cycle where poor people are hit hard and the ground for revolution is well prepared.

To Marx, the role of trade unions is the revolutionary overthrow of capitalist system. The ultimate purpose of unions is emancipating the worker from the degrading status of a wage slave. Trade unions are schools of socialism and organizing centers, which impart training to the workers and prepare them for their historic mission.

The unions have to carry out daily battle against employer for higher wages, better working conditions etc. but this immediate purpose is entirely incidental to the broader political purpose of uniting all workers against capitalism.

Marx argued that the workers could acquire class political consciousness only from outsiders who are away from economic struggle and from the areas of relations between the workers and capitalist employers. But for the purpose of complete and permanent emancipation of workers there has to be a political revolution. It is the intellectuals who must provide leadership to the struggle of the working class, not only for favourable terms of sale of labour power, but also for the abolition of the social system which compels property-less class to sale itself. To the rich class, Marx insisted that the unions should not adopt conservative narrow approach such as "a fair day's wage for a fix day's work". But they must aim at the total. "Abolition of the wage system" as a whole.

Thus Marx believes that trade unionism is characterized by inherent conflict between the capitalist and workers. As such the origin of unionism lies in the capitalist system. As long as trade unions are willing to be guided along the path of revolutionary transformation of society, their rule is progressive. In order to achieve and maintain permanent gains it is necessary for the unions to have a well-established socialist state.

Thus the trade union is viewed as a revolutionary and political organization. Its goal is social and political revolution and to capture the government. The unions believe in direct actions like strike, bundhs, gheraos, violence etc. in many countries such as UK, France, Australia labour parties with the help of trade unions have formed governments, and political power to avoid exploitation of the working class.

(1) ***Gandhian Theory:*** Gandhiji's philosophy is based on the principle of Survodaya and truth, Non-violence and trusteeship where class harmony is common. He argues that the trade unions are reformist organizations and economic institutions to be based on the supplementary role of both capital and labour.

Gandhiji insisted that the Trade Unions should not only concentrate upon improving economic condition of the workers but also try to raise the moral and intellectual standards of member and bring about all-round development through internal efforts. They should undertake teaching supplementary occupations to their members so as to reduce uncertainly of employment during strikes.

According to Gandhiji trade unions are not anti-capitalists because the idea is to take from capita, the labour's due share and nothing more, not by paralyzing capital but by labour reforms and by their self-consciousness and promoting internal relation of their self-restraint. The basic aim of union is not political but it is internal reforms and evolution of internal strength. At the later stage it may aspire for political goal.

Gandhiji argued that, it is proper to insist upon workers rights and principles, it is essential that the workers also recognize obligation that every right carries with it. The worker should treat business as their own and should pay proper attention to develop it in co-operation it in co-operation with the owner of business unit.

Gandhiji did not support unions taking part in political activities because of two reasons. Firstly because workers were neither properly trend nor enlightened and secondly political parties may exploit their unions for their own interest. He insisted that these strikes should be sympathetic strikes, which should be organized in sympathy of workers who are striking for just cause when all other means of setting the disputes were exhausted and a path of non-violence is followed strictly. Strikes should be adopted only when legitimate means of setting the disputes were tried. Gandhiji insisted on using the moral appeals fail, resorts to voluntary arbitration.

Gandhiji advised workers to organize themselves in orders to have more strength, in terms of wealth and resources through their labour than the capitalists through their money.

Types of Trade Unions

Since the days of industrialization till today, there has been a wide variety of trade unions in the world. These types have been classified in various ways.

According to Motives

(*i*) Paper unions

(*ii*) Ad Hoc unions.

According to their structure

(*i*) Craft union

(*ii*) Industrial union

(*iii*) General union

(*iv*) Staff union

According to the area of operation

(*i*) Local union

(*ii*) National union.

According to purpose

(*i*) *Reformist unions*

(*a*) Business unions

(*b*) Friendly or uplift unions.

(*ii*) *Revolutionary unions*

(*a*) Anarchist unions

(*b*) Political unions

(*c*) Predatory unions.

Let us discuss them briefly as follows:

(1) ***Paper Unions:*** Some unions are established to raise voice political field or to get a platform or have merely the status of unions. These unions are in record only on paper. In practice, they are not seen working in any field. In India about one fourth of the registered trade unions are just paper unions.

(2) ***Ad-Hoc Unions:*** Some unions may be established to secure some definite purpose or immediate objective such as strike-committees or action-committees. They may have huge membership for some time still a specific purpose is achieved. Soon its membership decreases as its utility or purpose is over. Some authors do not consider such unions as trade unions in real sense of the term.

(3) ***Craft Unions:*** A craft union is an organization of workers employed in particular craft or trade. It is also known as occupational union. Such organizations include those workers having similar skills, training and specialization. These are common among non-manual employees and professional workers. For example: the unions of bank employees, journalists, teachers, engineers, doctors etc. The member of their unions are craft-conscious rather than class-conscious and their unions aim at protecting the interests of the members although they provide barest minimum of associative integration. Such organizations are horizontal in nature as they include workers engaged in one process or group of processes only.

(4) ***Industrial Unions:*** It is an organization of the employees in a single industry without any distinction of occupation, sex, skills etc. its membership is relatively longer and the members are class conscious and feeling of solidarity is higher. For example, Rashtriya Mill Mazdoor Sangh for all textile workers in Mumbai. These organizations are vertical in nature because they cover all type of workers engaged in the same industry.

(5) ***General Unions:*** It is an organization of employees irrespective of their trade or craft. It is open to all classes of workers, which is the source of their strength and possess solidarity. For example, the Bombay Labour Union. It is suitable for employees in small concerns like hotels, commercial establishment etc.

(6) ***Staff Unions:*** It refers both craft and industrial unions. Its membership is of non-manual workers like clerks, supervisors etc. as tertiary sector increases, such types of unions will increase rapidly.

(7) ***Local Unions:*** These unions take more interest in local problems and try to solve them. Their operations are restricted to the smaller areas covering one or few cities or industrial centers.

(8) ***National Unions:*** These are the unions functioning at the national level and usually handle national problems faced by majority of the employees in the country.

(9) ***Reformist Unions:*** This type of unions are mainly interested in modifying or reforming the existing

structures and functioning of the unions rather than bringing about comprehensive changes in social economic and political structure of the economy. For example, they may insist on improving the working conditions and enforcing safety measure, increase in wage rates of the employees, providing training facilities etc. they undertake several measures like co-operative activities, insurance schemes, educational programmes etc. that will help workers to increase their efficiency and productivity and ability to earn more income and enjoy better status and higher standard of living. They takes steps to improve the dignity of labour by making the public and its leaders aware about the crucial role being played by labour class in modern society. Most of the unions in USA are of this type. Hoxie has further divided these unions on the basis of their objectives as Business Unions and Uplift Unions.

(i) *Business Unions:* These unions are formed and maintained mainly to represent workers in collective bargaining with their employees. They are more interested in the business activities hence they are mostly craft-conscious. They also undertakes measures for improving socio-economic conditions of their objectives. They insist a collective bargaining, voluntary arbitration, avoid strikes and political actions, as far as possible. But when all other measures fail they may adopt strikes and political actions to protect and promote their interests.

(ii) *Uplift or Friendly Unions:* These unions are more idealistic by nature and aim at elevating the moral, intellectual and social life of the workers. They may prepare idealistic plans for socio-economic development of their members. They also insist on demanding more facilities. Regarding education, health, recreation and entertainment, insurance and other benefits. These unions are not craft-conscious but are interest-conscious. They are conservative in nature and function within the legal limits to the benefit of the workers. They may be easily attracted towards political action, promoting co-operative ventures, participating in profit sharing schemes and other idealistic plan.

(10) *Revolutionary Unions:* Revolutionary unions aim at bringing about revolutionary way of destroying the existing structure completely and developing new institutions according to their ideals to be preferable for protecting interests of the workers. They aim at destroying capitalist institutions and structures, to abolish wage system and the institution of private property, to end the society. These unions are very much class-conscious and are ready to take any step essential to protect the interests of their members.

Hoxie has sub-divided their unions into the following types.

(a) *Anarchist Unions:* These unions aim at destroying the existing economic system by revolutionary means to establish socialist societies.

(b) *Political Unions:* These unions aim at gaining political power through political actions. They insist on enactment of the laws to eliminate power of capitalists and to redistribute income and wealth more equitable. They also aim at increasing the power and prestige of the working class in the society.

(c) *Predatory Unions:* These unions are dominated by gangsters and are ready to adopt violent means to achieve their goals. They have neither any lasting ideology nor any policy to adopt particular means to achieve their goals. They never worry about ethical of moral aspects of their actions and adopt ruthless methods and any measures to achieve results. Such unions are tools for increasing power of their leaders at any cost. These unions are further classified into a Hold-up Union of unscrupulous business agents and workers aiming at exploiting the consumers mainly for the benefit of their leaders.

The second type is Guerrilla Union which resorts to terrorism to enforce their demands. They do not trust in co-operation and peaceful means. They are anti-democratic and have ruthless and irresponsible leadership. They may use frequently, all sorts of violence for the purpose of exploiting the society at large.

(d) *Dependent Unions:* These are the unions, which are dependent partly or wholly on the other employees or the unions on their own. They do not like to take any risk unless they are assured of the full support by other unions or workers.

Impact of Globalization, Liberalization on Trade Union Movement in India

Trade Unions have been important institutions of industrial society. They have contributed significantly towards improvement of living standards of the workers and promoting equity and justice all over the world. Recent globalization and liberalization policies adopted by the most of the Governments have tended to pose several challenges to unions but at the same time it provides them opportunities to play a far effective and politically important role in the society.

Globalization has led to intense competition in product markets, accelerated mobility of capital and added to the vulnerability of labour.

Technological progress made if possible to reshape the production process through new forms of industrial organization, including and spatial reorganization of productive systems.

There are also changes in the skill composition of the work force along with large-scale entry of women into labour markets.

While trade unions all over the world have suffered less of membership account of crumbling trade barriers and globalize production. Recent changes in political and economic environment have made negative effects on the position and influence of trade employment away from large enterprises, on account of technological changes.

Flexible labour market policies have gained legitimacy and political support in the climate of economic liberalism. Practices such as subcontracting, outsourcing and the hiring of temporary and part-time workers, long considered as a typical employment, are becoming increasingly common especially at the lower end of the labour markets. The active welfare state committed to full employment and emphasizing expansionary economic policies did not continue beyond 1970's. In contrast the same state is withdrawing itself from the domain of employment and income policies and governments are moving away from and direct involvement in creation of jobs. The new policy concentrates on the governance of institutions to ensure functioning of markets.

Globalisation has made deep impact on workers and their organizations. Recently it has been noticed that there has been shift away from inward looking industrialization strategies, break from paternalistic industrial relations and rise in labour militancy. The rise in competitive pressure both in internal and external markets led to adoption of liberalized policies which was reflected from the more away from inward looking industrialization and protectionism towards export oriented industries and free trade policies. The state is withdrawing itself from production activities and calls private sector to enter the sphere reserved for public sector.

Trade unions have to adopt strategies to meet the needs of changing environment. This calls for going beyond traditional demands of wages working conditions and non-wage benefits met through organization and collective bargaining.

(A) ***Building the Membership Base:*** Webster and Adier observe that unions all over the world are surrounded by greater liberalization of economic and political regimes which hold out prospect for creating new rules of the game compelling key social actors which include government, organized labour, business and in some cases community organizations to negotiate and conclude agreements on major economic and social policies. When social interests are mediated by democratic regimes there is an opportunity to resolve the tensions that the likely to raise due to economic liberalization and to negotiate a compromise solution. However the capacity of unions to influence the course of events depends on their strengths and support among unionized and unorganized sections of society. Membership campaigns organized by union's aim at making unions stronger.

(B) ***Recognition of Trade Union Structures:*** The new economic environment calls for reorganization of the structures of trade unions it may include:

(*i*) Decentralization and adaptation of unions to new forms of industrial organization.

(*ii*) Creation of new union structures to ensure representation of workers in the spatially decentralization units of production.

(*iii*) Measures to ensure the financial viability of unions, which take on new responsibilities to provide services to the members.

(*iv*) Centralization and co-ordination on union functions through merges and alliances at national and sectoral level.

Regarding decentralization and adaptation to new forms of organizations of the unions it may be stated that, as the benefits of liberalization filtered down to employees at the higher level of skill spectrum, the orientation of workers have shifted to economic issues and there has been a gradual decline in radical political unionism. There is rise in economic unionism demanding improved benefits at enterprise level. The new structures have been useful to deliver better wages and fringe benefits, but only for a small group as compared to the previous structures which were able to serve larger number of workers in an environment of greater militancy and class solidarity.

Now decentralized bargaining along with independent company union, which are not affiliated to apex, bodies or political parties have become common practice in India especially since 1980's of under conditions of the regional disparities in income distribution.

An outstanding feature of unionism in developing countries has been the divergence of interests between the two extremes of a vastly polarized labour force. According to Bhattacharjee, this makes it difficult for unions to combine traditional wage bargaining with their new role of giving voice and representation to workers at the plant level. The dominant trend in India has been rapid growth of company unions which are not affiliated to political parties, nor apex bodies.

As decentralized and geographically dispersed units of production are not viable in terms of size and location of unionizing workers. Here has been inverse relationship between the cost unionization the size of enterprises, which calls for a new approach to organizational structures that can maximize the benefits of unionization. A close look at the union structures in developing countries especially in India indicates at tendency to separate the bargaining and voice functions, which has margin implications for future strategies. But such separation of bargaining and voice functions implies further deterioration in income distribution which unions cannot afford in developing economies because "any society, which has bones deep inequalities in income distribution, tends to limit the functioning of redistributive institutions. Trade unions in such societies may not be able to perform there as providers of social cohesion. Thus serious efforts are required to prevent any deterioration of income inequalities in developing countries, and accordingly trade unions should develop new strategies.

(c) ***Initiating Collective action for Institutional benefits:*** According to A.V. Jose "Union capacity to deliver successful outcomes depends on whether workers right interests have been incorporated into legislation or other regulatory instruments of the labour market".

Labour legislation, collective agreements, social security and minimum wages etc. indicate the strength and influence of trade unions. In developing countries unions have made good progress in maintaining and upgrading statutory safeguards on employment and working condition. But such gains are restricted to workers in organized formal sector.

The main task for unions today is to build distributive institutions to protect interest of workers especially in the unorganized informal sector. This can be achieved through the following measures.

(*i*) Macro level framework agreements covering.

(*ii*) Minimum standard of employment.

(*iii*) Minimum wage.

(*iv*) Portable benefits including healthcare and safety measures, irrespective of location of employment.

In this context the unions should possess empowerment to quarantine a secured income and decent working conditions for all.

"Trade Unions as representatives of a very organized and articulate group of society". Have a historic mandate to defend and promote human rights. In order to achieve this, unions need to move beyond their customary role of defending civil and political rights. Union priorities in this field include appropriate human rights programmes in collaboration with other actors in society.

Jose concludes, "A politically important option in the coming decades will be to build on its established role in safeguarding social cohesion. This implies strategic orientation to the long-term goals of security, equity and justice for all in the world of work. The above goals are attainable through redistributive transfers, specially aimed at connecting income inequalities and raising the level of social consumption. The strategies for reaching the goals need to be anchored in the mobilization of diverse interest groups in society on a political platform". The long-term objectives of labour movement in developing societies is continuous pursuit of the redistributive policies and programmes.

Thus it may be concluded that today in a period of economic reforms where productivity and competitiveness are indispensable. It is clearly a matter of life and death for both management and workers unions to redesign their approaches to suit this changes environment. The unions have to develop awareness among workmen about the significance of present economic reforms.

Similarly management must realize that there own future and that of their plant depends on the active co-operation of the workmen and their leadership development among the workmen and should organize suitable programmes for this purpose. Thus a new work culture has to be developed which will help the plant to survive in the new competitive climate.

Origin and Historical Development of Trade Union (movement) in India

The main elements of the development of Trade Union in different parts of world are more or less similar. As a result of Industrial Revolution, factory system, division of labour, developments lead to the significant changes in the working and living condition of the workers, and the whole society got itself divided into wage-earners proletariat and capitalists or bourgeoisie classes. Thus the workers had no alternative except to sale their labour to earn livelihood. Under the atmosphere dominated by lassie faire policy on government was ready to interfere in day today matters of economy. This provided must fertile ground for the capitalists to exploit the labour and make huge profits to the invested for expanding the scale of production. In order to protect themselves from the miserable working and living conditions and continuous of their service by attaining equally balanced position with the management. When the joint action failed, the practices evolved by the workers were joint withdrawal from the work. It was this labour protest on an organized scale through the support of philanthropic personalities and liberal social thinkers that organized labour unions came into existence firstly in England. Soon labour unions were formed in several countries of the world where India was no exception.

The growth and development of Trade Union Movement or Labour Movement in India originated around 1875 and made steady progress during later period. On the basis of tendencies reflected by the movement, it can be divided into the following periods for the purpose of detailed study.

Social Welfare Period (1875-1918)

The first Cotton Mill was established in Bombay in 1854 and the first Jute Mill in Bangalore in 1855 and the development of factory system of production began in India. The development of factory system in India led to the social evils like employment and exploitation of women and child labour on one hand and worsening of working condition, completely indifferent attitude on the part of the government, on the other. There were no means available to the workers to create public opinion to get support in their attempt to make the society aware about hardships and suffering of the working class. Most of the workers were of rural origin coming to Bombay in search of employment, illiterate, submissive and unorganized, there were no attempts of collective bargaining or obtaining redress through concerted action. The workers had to change the job by joining other industry or go back to their village. Under such conditions some of the workers like Sorabjee Shapurji Bengali (1875) and N.M. Lokhanday (1884) tried to attract the attention of the government towards unhealthy working conditions of the workers and demanded early legislation to protect their interests. At the same time mill owners of Lancashire forced the British government to restrict employment of women and child labour in Indian factories to protect themselves from very cheap Indian goods. So the British government passed the first Indian Factories Act in 1881 which was amended in 1891 and 1911 to incorporate certain changes regarding working hours, conditions of work for women and children etc. the other important development supporting the development of Trade Unionism in India, during this period were.

(*i*) The investigation of Meade Moor (1874)
(*ii*) The Factory Commission (1875)
(*iii*) The Factory Act (1881)
(*iv*) The Second Bombay Factory Commission (1884)
(*v*) The workers meeting in Bombay (1884) and submission of a memorial to the Commission
(*vi*) Investigation by Jones (1890)
(*vii*) Holding mass meeting in Bombay (1890)
(*viii*) Submission of another memorial to the government signed by about 17000 workers.

All these developments stimulated the infant labour movement to grow rapidly. As a response to the memorial the mill owners agreed to grant a weekly holiday to the workers.

In 1890, Bombay Millhands Association was established by Shri N.M. Lokhanday to provide a clearing-house for the grievances of the workers and to draw public attention towards the problems of the workers. Shri Lokhanday organized a meeting of about 10,000 workers in Bombay and presented certain demands of workers and place before the employers and authorities, the legitimate grievances of the workers he started publishing a new paper known as DINBANDHU.

Later on several unions were also formed, which included:

(*i*) "The Amalgamated Society of Railway Servants in India and Burma (for European and Anglo Indian railway/ employees) (1891)" was established and registered under Companies Act to serve their own interests.

(*ii*) The Printers Union of Kolkata (1905).

(*iii*) The Bombay Postal Union, followed by Kolkata and Chennai (1907).

(*iv*) Kamgar Hitawardha Sabha (1909).

(*v*) The Social Service League (1910).

These were loose or general organizations and the leaders were mostly social reformers from the Moderate School of politics. The main objectives of these unions were to promote literacy among the factory workers, redress their grievances through constitutional means and promote welfare activities on a wider scale. These organizations although aimed at improving the socio-economic conditions of the workers, still they were not labour unions in the real sense of the term. They were also not affiliated to any central organization or federation. They served the purpose of attracting the attention of the public and government towards the need of improving working conditions in the factories. They also provided necessary background for the establishment of labour union on sound lines.

During this period employers also realized the need for organizing their unions to protect their common interests which needed common action. During the period 1879-1881 the employers established the following organizations:

(*i*) The Bombay and Bengal Chamber of Commerce.

(*ii*) The Bombay Mill-owners Association.

(*iii*) The Calcutta Traders Association.

(*iv*) The Indian Jute Manufacturers' Association.

(*v*) The Indian Chamber of Commerce.

(*vi*) The British Indian Association.

The organization of the employers were mainly interested in keeping the wheels of the factory moving and to earn maximum return of the investments. So they resisted formation of strikes and were keen in removing the persons who participated or motivated others to participate in strikes. However most of their organizations could not survive over longer period.

Early Trade Union Period (1918-1924)

According to V.V. Giri, this period was characterized by a new era and the era of growth and the leadership of trade union during this period was passed on to the politicians from the social workers. The movement took deeper roots in India after the World War I because of several reasons. For example, at the end of the war profits and prices went up but the wages lagged far behind. It deteriorated the standard of living of the workers and industrial unrest increased. The economic discontent resulted into strikes in textile industry. Secondly the success of Russian Revolution of 1971 served as an ideal for the workers and they realized that the exploitation of workers could be controlled by political revolution. The Communist party in India became very popular and it could control AITUC in 1925. Thirdly in ILO was established in 1919 that gave status to the working class and provided opportunity to bring labour leaders from various countries on common platform to discuss their issues and pass resolutions which were binding on the member countries. After the war several Indian soldiers were compelled to join labour market as there was no alternative opportunity available for employment. Gandhi's Civil Disobedience movement during 1920-21 provided support to the demands of the workers and it provided young but dedicated leaders to the infant Trade Union movement. Thus political element became dominant in Indian trade union movement right from its early days. During this period a large number of unions were established such as the GIP Railway Workers Union, Bombay Railwaymen's Union, the Madras Textile Labour Union, the Jamshedpur Labour Association, Indian Seamen's Union etc.

The workers organization spread rapidly throughout India especially in cotton textile and jute industries, railways and transport services. However a large number of unions were loose organizations and they could not function on permanent basis. Their emphasis on short-term gains like increase in wages made them like strike committees, which stopped functioning immediately as their short-term goal was achieved.

The political leaders who participated in Indian Trade Union movement include Motilal Nehru, Jawaharlal Nehru, Subhash Chandra Bose, S.A. Dange, V.V. Giri etc.

Left Wing Trade Union Period (1924-1935)

From the early stages the Indian Trade Unions movement and communists held Moscow Trade Unions as their ideals who brought about violent strikes. The Communist Unions captured AITUC and the union leaders were prosecuted in Kanpur in 1924 and Meerut in 1929. The rapid growth of the Trade Unions was the result of several factors such as,

(*i*) Repressive measures and violence adopted by the British Government, indiscriminate arrests and imprisonment of political leaders.

(*ii*) Higher profits earned by the employer in face of falling real wages.

(*iii*) Growth of independence movement.

(*iv*) Increase in misery, poverty and unemployment of the workers on a large-scale during the great depression.

However instead of tracing the challenges the Trade Union movement started disintegrating on political basis. In 1926-27 several workers and peasants organization developed and in 1928, All-india Workers and Peasant's Party was formed by the union of their local parties. This resulted into increase in domination of Meftist parties in Indian Trade unions and a large number of strikes took places. The dominance of communist led the government longest trials the Meerut conspiracy case under which several union leaders were arrested. The trial aimed at crushing the movement.the movement was divided into two types Leftists and Rightists, which differed on the question of international polities. Rightists resisted the policy of strikes, militant actions and insisted that the unions should concentrate as economic issues and not a political action. The Leftists held the view that the trade unions are basically workers organizations and their aim is to establish socialism in place of capitalism through revolution of proletariat. Unless economic issues are supplemented with political action it is not possible to capture political power.

During early thirties the Trade Union movement was characterized by disunity. There were three main unions.

(*i*) The ALTUC led by the militant nationalists and Royalists.

(*ii*) The All India Trade Union Federation (ALTUF) led by compress nationalists and moderates.

(*iii*) The Red Trade Union Congress (RTUC) led by the communists aimed at the establishment of the dictatorship of proletariat. In addition there were few other organizations such as Textile Labour Association (TLA), All India Railway Men's Federation etc. having their own methods and policies.

Trade Union's Unity Period (1935-1939)

As economic depression started disappearing and employer started the practices of rationalization and wage reduction in order to minimize the cost of production. This resulted into increases in labour unrest and also the rise in union membership. The workers leaders realized that the division of the movement was very costly for the workers. A large number of strikes took place so that in 1934 the total number of mom days lost increased to 47.7 lakhs against 21.7 lakhs in 1933. Labour leaders thought that unity is most eventual for labour unions. In 1935 RTUC and ALTUC merger took place and ALTUC was recognized as the central organization and the principles of one union for one industry and class struggle were accepted. It was also decided that the affiliation with any foreign organization was prohibited and a delegate to attend the international Labour conference was to be elected on the basis of majority in the annual session of the Trade Union confers, are the right of free propaganda and criticism to every party within the unified organization were also granted.

In 1937 general elections the Congress government came into power in seven states. The inauguration of Provincial Autonomy and the greater freedom of the workers full support of the Congress government stimulated rapid increase in the membership of the unions. The NTUF merged with the ALTUC and nearly after a decade of split. The trade union unity took place around 1940. As Punekar observed, during the decade of 1930-40 Indian trade unionism was divided house and the average industrial worker kept himself aloof from organized union.

The Second World War Period (1939-1946)

During the Second World War the Indian economy has to face several stresses and strains. AITUC had several political fractions emphasizing different roles India should play in the war. A Radical Democratic Party insisted that the AITUC should participate in the anti fascist war. The other group led by S.C. Bose and others opposed the view of the Redicals as they consider that it was the imperialist war of Great Britain with which India has no concern. So the Radicals left the AITUC and formed the Indian Federation of Labour.

The developments in the political field also affected Indian Trade Union Movement. The Indian National Congress declared the policy of non co-operation and initiated Quit India Movement in 1992. Several political leaders were arrested. Hence Communist dominance in the AITUC increased significantly, several factors were responsible for raising the status of trade unions in India. There include:

(*i*) Recognition of Trade Unions by many Indian Industrialist.

(*ii*) Increase in welfare measures by the Government and the employees to increase production of war materials and other essential goods.

(*iii*) Ban on strikes and lock-out during war period.

(*iv*) A Tripartitle Labour Conference was convened in 1942 for the first time to provide Common platform discussion and understanding each other's views between workers and the employees. On account of favourable environment, the membership as well as the number of trade unions increased rapidly which reached to around 865 units and 8.89 lakh members in 1944-45.

When the war ended, there were three major unions based on the political ideology. The Communists dominated ALTUC while the Royalist controlled Indian Federation of Labour while the Socialists and Nationalists were trying to buildup labour front in Ahmedabad and Jamshedpur. However, Indian Unions could improve their abilities to participate in negotiations with employers and participate with confidence in the tripartite deliberations in order to protect the interest of the working class.

The Post Independence Period (1947 onwards)

The deteriorating economic conditions of workers as a result of rise in the cost of living made workers aware of the need of organizing their to secure relief hence the number of unions increased rapidly. As the attempts to restructure ALTUC failed, those who believed in the ideals different than those of the ALTUC separated and a new union named the Indian National Trade Union was formed in May, 1947. Soon the INTUC became the largest federation of trade union and hence the most representative organization of workers in India. The main objective of the INTUC was to find out the solutions of labour problems by peaceful means.

After Independence a new political party known as Socialist Party was formed and another labour organization known as Hind Mazdoor Sabha also was established in 1948. The Indian Federation of Labour merged into it. Some other groups formed the United Trade Union Congress (UTUC). The government recognized these central organizations of workers for the purpose of representation for consultation and national as well as international representation. As Jan Sangh emerged as a separate political party, the Bhartiya Mazdoor Sangh (BMS) was formed in 1955. Similarly with the formation SSP party, a union known as Hind Mazdoor Panchayat (HMP) was established in 1962. The Communist Pary-Marxist formed the Centre of Indian Trade Unions (CITU). The UTUC was split and another organization UTUC Leninsarani came into existence. After the split of the Indian National Congress the new Congress in 1972 decided to affiliate all trade unions under its leadership with National Labour Organization (NLU). In addition, there are several unions who are members of these federations and also affiliated to other central organizations. Some unions and their federations prefer to operate as separate units although sometimes they may collaborate with one or the other organization.

Several attempts are being made since 1952 to promote unity in the labour movement. Similarly INTUC, AITUC and HMS tried to achieve unity at the apex level by way of formation of National Council of Central Trade Unions (NCCTU), but this attempt was able to achieve only partial success.

After the declaration of the Emergency the INTUC, AITUC and the HMS combined and joined with the representatives of the employees to form the National Apex body. But when the emergency was lifted and Janata Party came into power, this body also disappeared.

Now Indian Trade Unions are not mere ad-hoc bodies or strike committees but are permanent organization fighting for the cause of working class. It's large number of political, economic, historical and international factors have helped Indian unions not only to become strong and permanent organizations, but also to get a legal status and to represent workers either to the government or to international organizations.

Indian Trade Unions have been allied with one or the other political parties not on the basis of partnership based on equality and independence as in England, but as mere adjuncts of the political parties. Thus, they are the handmade of the political parties Indian trade unions although suffer from rivalries still they have been able to influence public policy and labour and industrial legislation. They were crucial in the process of development suitable machinery of joint consultation for negotiating various issues between labour and management.

According to Memoria and others the significant changes in unions have been manifested in three ways.

1. There has developed distinction between political leaders with secondary interest in labour union activity

and labour leaders with a secondary political interest. More emphasis is being paid to labour leadership by giving more attention to the improvement of union cadres, finances and training in official administration.

2. The national federations have shown greater interest in long-term activities in order to strengthen personnel and organizational aspects of the trade unions. Now Trade Union Federation arranges training programmes for the workers.
3. It has been realized that now unions should function as autonomy institutions rather than as appendages of political parties.

Problems Faced Trade Unions

Indian Trade Union Movement has made significant progress in India. They have been successful in improving the socio-economic conditions of the workers. However, the progress has neither been adequate nor smooth. In terms of quality the performance is not satisfactory. On account of several problems, the movement has remained weak. Some of the major problems of the Trade Unions may be summarized as follows:

Small Size and Low Membership

During last six decades, the size of the trade unions in India has been steadily decreasing. The average membership of unions which was around 4000 during 1920's has decreased among workers, trade unions are being established in smaller plants. Thus, in face of increase in the number of unions and union membership, average membership, of individual unions is decreasing. Secondly the rivalry among the union leaders and the central organizations has resulted into multiplicity of unions leading to reduction in average size of the union. It implies that trade unionism gives berth to more and more leaders rather than becoming forum for increasing number of workers. Thus, it fails to cement the bonds of workers with unions, which is not a healthy sign. It is also stated that, on account of the average number of workers employed per factory level tends to remain very low. Hence it is necessary to change the primary unit of unionization from a factory to industry only the small size of unions and low membership reduces their viability, dependence, lack of purposiveness and coherence and financially weaker ones.

Weak Finances of the Unions

The primary source of income of the unions is the subscription of members and other dues. It accounts for about 70 per cent of the total income. The other sources like donations, special collection etc. Accounts for a very small percentage of the total income. The main reason of poor financial position of the unions is inadequate strength of membership due to small size of unions. Even the rate of contribution is also very small. In case of several unions, it is observed that the union fees even at these low rates, are not regularly paid by the workers in spite of huge time and energy of the leaders being spent as collecting them, mostly on account of lower wage rates and the spendthrift have of the workers and also the lack of commitment of the workers to the unions, as the services rendered by the unions fail to impress upon the members that the unions can play important role in their work life. Due to lack of finances the Unions cannot introduce schemes for the benefit of the working class. The unions also cannot maintain full-time paid efficient staff. The unions cannot develop reserve funds and their bargaining power tends to remain very weak. Thus, it is the result of vicious circle as the equality of the services is poor because the contribution is poor and vice-versa.

Limited Area and Uneven Growth

Trade unionism in India is mostly confined to the organized sector, which is urban in character. This sector covers the workers employed in registered factories, mines, plantation, government and quasi-government bodies, ports, insurance etc. factory labour constitutes less than 2.5 per cent of the labour force, while the entire organized work force constitutes less than 10 per cent of the labour force. The trade union activities are concentrated in large-scale industries and that also to manual labour only. Indian unionism has been concentrated in a few states and in bigger industrial centers as nearly 70 per cent of the unions are located in six industrially developed states. Thus although the trade unionism has taken roots in India, they have developed unevenly and in a limited area both geographically and industry-wise.

Dominance of Outsiders in Union

Indian unionism has been led by the outsiders right from the early days, on account illiteracy, poverty and ignorance of the workers. The presence of outsiders results into political unionism. Although the outsiders have made significant contributions towards development of unionism, still outsiders are observed to be more prone to cause disturbance of industrial peace and as the outsiders have either political links or other extraneous considerations, the union potential is not fully utilized for protecting interests of the workers. As the outside leaders have to look after the activities of many unions in different plants at the same time, they may fail to pay proper attention to the problems of the unions. They may fail to project the workers problems before the government or management. The political leaders use unions for maximizing their own interests rather than maximizing the wages for the workers. Thus political unionism leading to allegiance of each union to a different political party results into multiplicity of unions and intra and inter union rivalry, low membership, unsound finances, lack of welfare activities, lack of strength and weaker bargaining power, thus vicious circle repeats by itself.

Multiplicity of Unions and Inter and Intra-union Rivalry

Outside leaders treated unions as their bases of power and in their struggle for more power, they have caused structural fragmentation of Indian Trade Union movement. Multiplicity of union and inter (among) and intra (within) union rivalry in the same bargaining territory are widespread. In addition, political rivalry among the outside leaders and political parties, the trade union law, conferring industrial relations rights upon unions with as few as only seven members etc. are responsible for the sorry state of affairs. Absence of statutory provision and management practice of according recognition to the multiplicity of unions and inter and intra-union rivalrics. Rcccntly, union rivalries based on political considerations have increased. The splitting of unions and the formation of new unions having sympathies with political parties has become common in union operations at different levels. In several industrial units, unions whether affiliated to central organization or not, tend to operate independently, each claiming to be representative of all the workers. Attempts are also made by the union to undermine the influence and image of the other raising questions about bona fide of rival readers. Under such conditions some clever employers may take advantage of the rivalries through playing one union against the other. Basically inter union conflicts arise on account of differences in the views about worker's interest and the means to be adopted for achieving them.

Similarly instances of Intra union rivalry are increasing in recent times. According to the National Commission on labour, healthy revelry and opposition is necessary for maintaining and increasing the strength of any democratic institution but it may have pernicious effects when motivated by personal consideration. The rivalry within the trade unions movement discouraged healthy and more stable development of trade unions.

The Problems of Recognition

It is the fundamental problems faced by the trade unionism. One peculiar characteristic of Indian Industrial Relations system is that the employers are not obliged to recognize any union, excepts in case of some states. The employers are reluctant to recognize voluntary the majority union on sole bargaining agent in a particular bargaining territory. The result is proliferation of large number of unions, mostly of small size, competing with each other for seeking recognition by the employer as majority union. This result into inter-union rivalry and leads to industrial strife.

As a result of the resistance on the part of management to recognize the union and the ambivalence on this issue on the part of the government, each competing union stresses its demand on the higher side so as to gain and maintain member loyalty. Secondly, the management prefer to settle the disputes through adjudication which obstructs the sound development of collective bargaining.

The solution to the problem of recognition lies in statutory provision for the compulsory recognition of a majority union as a sole bargaining agent and providing a detailed procedure for determining the majority union.

Union Security

Under union security provision an argument is made with the employer regarding not to employ a non-member.

There are two forms about it.

(*a*) Under the Closed Shop Scheme, employer recruits only union members. It gives the union full control over the supply of labour.

(*b*) In case of Union Shop arrangement new entrants to employment, if they are not members of the union, they must join the union, they must join the union within specified period.

In India, there is no such provision either in the statutes nor is there any such practice. Such a practice is essential for strengthening a stable union. It will help in removing the interference by the employers in union activities and will make employment of the members more secure and may help in creating and developing internal leadership. However, such a policy may infringe the right of freedom of association; hence the union may lose its voluntary character.

(*c*) Check off is another element of union security. According to this system the employer deducts union subscription or dues from the wages of the employees for handing over it to the union. However such a practice will be illegal in India because such a deduction is not authorized under the Payment of wages Act, 1936.

Neglect of Worker's Welfare

On account of shortage of funds, ignorance of the workers and migratory character of the employees making unstable labour force, trade union have not given proper attention towards welfare facilities of the workers such as providing medical and sickness relief, educational and cultural facilities etc. instead, trade unions have become fighting units of political parties and act like strike committees. Hence the Unions have failed to inspire faith among their members, develop committed membership and command loyalty from workers.

Defective Administration

The administrative aspect of several unions has been far from satisfactory. As the proper conduct of the affairs of the unions remains absent, the functioning of the worker's body cannot be expected to be healthy and efficient.

Taking into consideration the different problems or weaknesses of Indian Trade Unionism, it may be concluded that we cannot expect the trade union movement to improve qualitatively. But it is also true that unless qualitative improvement takes place the future of Indian Trade Unionism with not be bright.

National Commission Labour for Strengthening Trade Unions (1969)

The NCL has made several recommendations on various aspects of Trade Unions for improving their strength, vitality and efficiency. These recommendations may be summarized as follows.

Enlargement of Functions

The NCL has emphasized that the unions must pay greater attention to the basic needs of its members, which are:

(*i*) To secure fair wages for the workers.

(*ii*) To safeguard security of tenure and improved conditions of service.

(*iii*) To enlarge opportunities for promotion and training.

(*iv*) To improve working and living conditions.

(*v*) To provide for educational, cultural and recreational facilities.

(*vi*) To co-operate in and facilitate technological advance by broadening the understanding of workers and it's underlying issues.

(*vii*) To promote identity of interests of the workers with their industry.

(*viii*) To offer responsible co-operation is improving levels of production and productivity, discipline, and high standard of quality.

(*ix*) To promote individual and collective welfare.

In addition the union should also undertake social responsibilities such as:

(*a*) Promotion of national integration.

(*b*) Influencing the socio-economic policies of the community through active participation in the formulation of these policies.

(*c*) Instilling in their members a sense of responsibility towards industry and community.

(*d*) The unions should co-operate and support development process in India.

Leadership

The NCL has strongly recommended that –

1. Steps should be taken to promote internal leadership and give it more responsible role to play.
2. Internal leadership should be kept outside the pale of victimization.
3. The permissible limit of outsider in the executive of the unions should be reduced to 25 per cent.
4. Ex-employees need not be treated as outsiders.
5. There should be no ban as non-employees holding a position in the executive of the union.

Union Rivalries

The NCL was of the opinion that once its recommendations are accepted regarding recognition of unions building up internal leadership, shift to collective bargaining, the institution of an independent authority for union recognition, would reduce inter union rivalries among unions significantly. The commission stated that intra union rivalries among unions significantly. The commission stated that inter union rivalries may be left for central organization concerned for settlement. If it fails to solve the disputes then a Labour Court should be set up for the purpose.

(a) ***Registration:*** The commission has recommended that the registration of the union should be cancelled it –

(1) Its membership falls below the minimum prescribed for registration.

(2) The union fails to submit its annual return.

(3) The union submits defective returns and defect will not be rectified within the prescribed time.

It also recommended that an application for re-registration should not be considered within six month from the date of cancellation of registration.

(b) ***Improvement of Financial Condition:*** For the purpose of improving financial position of the unions the commission recommended that the membership fee should be raised to Rs. 10 per month in place of Rs. 2 at present. It did not favour the present practice of collecting Rs. 10 per cent or even more as membership fee because it would lead to raising different amounts within each slab for the same-group of workers.

(c) ***Verification of Membership:*** The Industrial Relations Commission should decide the representative character of a union either by way of examination of membership records or by holding an election by secret ballot open to all employers.

(d) ***Recognition of the Unions:*** The NCL stated that, "It would be desirable to make recognition compulsory under a central law in all undertakings employing 100 or more workers or where the capital invested above a stipulated size. A trade union seeking recognition as a bargaining agent from an individual employer should have a membership of at least 30 per cent of workers in that establishment. The minimum membership should be 25 per cent, if recognition is sought for an industry in a local area. Where more unions than one contend for recognition, the unions having the layer following should be recognized.

In addition the following measures may be suggested:

(i) ***Strong Union:*** In order to protect and promote interest of the workers a strong union having equal bargaining power to that of the management is necessary. According to V.V. Giri, "if the trade union movement is not united and strong enough to achieve its objective, then industrial structure to be built in India on the basis of full-fledged socialist democracy would not have firm foundation and the state, in spite of its best ideals and designs would find it difficult to assure fundamental rights to the working class".

The other measures include –

(ii) Eliminating unhealthy political influence.

(iii) To follow the principle of one union on industry.

(iv) To train the workers about their responsibilities.

(v) The maintenance of strike funds by the unions is necessary especially to pay the strike-pay during period of prolonged strikes.

(vi) Educating workers in the field of management of trade unionism.

(vii) Developing united labour front with one policy objective and programme and method.

(viii) The Trade Union Act, 1956 should be amended and

(a) The minimum number of members required to form trade union should be increased from 7 to 50 per cent of the employers of organization.

(b) The scope of outside leadership should be reduced from 50 per cent to 10 per cent.

(c) The Act should make provision for avoiding dual membership.

(d) There should be legal provision for recognition of representative unions.

(*ix*) Trade unions should be so developed that they should be able to form a labour party so that labour unions can have adequate strength both in the industry and parliament.

(*x*) The central organization should publish journals to make Trade Union movement effective.

Developing Work Culture

Trade Unions have the responsibility of developing work culture among workers by inculcating sense of discipline and responsibility about their normal duties; along with their rights and privileges.

Amalgamation

In India at present there is a huge number of small unions having membership less than 500. Hence they suffer from weak organization, finance support and leadership, which result into weakening the base of movement. Hence it is desirable to amalgamate small units for attaining stability and growth. If necessary the Trade Union Act may be amended.

Change in Employer's Attitude

In order to make Trade Union movement successful and effective there is need to bring about change in the attitude of the employers. The employers must realize the benefits of collective bargaining for attaining and maintaining industrial peace.

Role of Trade Unions in Increasing Productivity in Industrial Organisations

Productivity is the relationship between the outputs and inputs used. It is not merely volume of output in relation to inputs used. It will be maximum when highest output is obtained with minimum expense on inputs. Productivity is the ratio of output to the input. In industrial undertaking productivity of labour and also of capital are important factors affecting effectiveness and efficiency of management.

According to Peter Drucker, continuous improvement of productivity is management's most important job. In developing country like India, productive has given top priority by all those who are concerned with it including the government because in a developing economy various factors like growth rate, national income, employment, inflation, standard of living of the people etc. depend upon the productivity. In order to promote productivity harmonious industrial relations are necessary. In a welfare state it's the direct responsibility of the government not only to protect the interests of the weaker sections of society like workers but also to maintain an atmosphere where production activities will continue smoothly in the economy. The history of industrial relations shows that on an average the mom days lost on account of strikes and lockouts work out at around Rs. 300 crores per year. It has been said that there are some gaps or defects in the Industrial Disputes Act, which make enforcement of the act ineffective. The interpretation of the definition of industry and workman by the courts of law has created several problems.

Productivity is the result of work norms procedures, time and motion studies, incentive and motivation systems etc. the key to the productivity lies in the proper motivation of the human factors of production, which include labour, trade unions and management. In the ultimate analysis it is the human element which decides to make optimum use of capital or not. Hence mere capital investment may not automatically lead to higher productivity. But as demonstrated by Hawthrone Experiments it is the human factor, which plays a key role in promoting productivity. Productivity of human resource deals with human behaviour patterns in industrial environments and also with the factors that motivate men, individually and in groups under favourable climate positive attitude towards productivity among the work force and supervisors help in improving productivity in the organization.

Role of Trade Unions in Increasing Productivity

It has been realized that human resource plays a key role in increasing productivity in an organization. In a broader context it may be argued that issue of improving productivity has been concern of all i.e. workers, framework be studied and government. The policy framework of the government and legal framework be studied and be made conductive to maintain healthy industrial relations. Most of the industrial disputes and conflicts arise on account of inadequate attention being paid to the development of human resources by the management. In order to get best out of each worker and to provide creative outlet to his potential, ideal policies for proper selection, training, promotion, motivation, work environment etc. need to be formulated and effectively implemented. Once employees realize that in the ultimate analysis their well being rests with the development of the origination. The feeling of belongingness on the part of employees has of motivation etc. measures so that maximum co-operation of the workers can be obtained and management can achieve the goals easily. Major problems that disturb the smooth process of production and affect productivity adversely are the outcome of pent-up emotions of workers based on their feeling that they are not getting fair deal and proper treatment by the superiors. The employees may have grievances whether real or imaginary, but they need to be properly attended by the management. It is desirable to develop an active and fast working grievance handling machinery in the organization so that workers can get satisfactory solutions to their grievances complaints and other problems.

At present Indian Trade Union Movement suffers from several limitations especially multiplicity of unions, infra and inter union rivalries, political interference, poor finances, selfish and short-sighted leadership etc. Hence in spite of good inventions on the part of management it becomes difficult to identify union for recognition for establishing sound relations. Hence it is suggested that it is desirable to take unions in confidence before any major decision is taken that will affect production, productivity and work environment of the organization. Trade unions should realize that they should produce a bigger cake before asking for a bigger share in the cake. The workers should be made aware about the fact, that higher productivity benefits not only to them but also to the organization and the society at large. It also helps to create good image of the organization in the eyes of the public. Even the workers may feel proud of working in such growth and social welfare oriented organization.

If productivity has to improve, then there has to be one union in one establishment as sole representative of workers. It is possible that clever management may take advantage of inter and intra rivalry. So workers should realize that "United we stand, divided we fall". It is also responsibility of both the workers and their unions to maintain discipline in the establishment so that the disputes and differences can be resolved amicably and peacefully without that the disputes and differences can not be resolved amicably and peacefully without disturbing the regular flow of production of goods in the organization. Trade union leaders are trained to take decision to promote interests of workers, organization and the nations, rather than pursuing personal and political interests. The main responsibility of trade unions lies in giving new orientation to their outlook and attitude towards industrial development itself. The trade union leaders should adopt positive attitude and negotiate with management to decide about sharing the gains of productivity and production, keeping some balance to be useful for expansion of the organization to generate employment opportunities in labour surplus economy. Acts of violence need to be avoided by workers, management and the government. Any breach of law is penalized according to the provisions of the law of the land. The Government should amend labour laws in order to make it suitable to handle current and potential problems.

Conciliation proceeding and adjudication procedures should be completed as early as possible, for restoring confidence of the employees and employers in the present functioning of industrial relations machinery. If necessary addition staff, labour court and industrial tribunals should be established to handle cases without delay. Labour laws need trade union movement strong and effective to contribute significantly towards achievement of not only the organizational goals but also the goals of economic development set for every Five-year Plan in India.

Law and Practice Relating to Recognition of Trade Union

According to S.C. Srivastava recognition of Trade Union is a backbone of collective bargaining. However in spite of the Government's policy to encourage trade unions, there is no central legislation on the subject. There are Voluntary Code of Discipline and Legislation in some of the states. On account of absence of any central legislation, management in some states, where legislation on recognition does not exist, refused flatly to recognize trade union on the following grounds.

(*a*) Most of the office bearers of the union were outsiders.

(*b*) The Trade Union keeps outsiders disapproved by management and particularly politicians and ex-employees.

(*c*) The union consisted of only small number of employees.

(*d*) These were in existence in many rival unions.

(*e*) The trade union was not registered under the Trade Union Act, 1926.

However these objections cannot be accepted because to accept them implies interference in the functioning of the trade unions. Thus refusal by the employers to recognize or bargain with Unions has been major obstacle to healthy and sound development of Trade Unionism and collective bargaining in India.

Historical Development of Recognition

The recognition is said to be oriented in relation to government and its servants. Before 1933 Government servants were prohibited from submitting collective memorials and petitions. Afterwards the right of recognition was granted only to combination, which confirmed certain rules. The Unions, which confirmed these rules, were allowed to conduct negotiating with government on behalf of their members.

(*a*) The Royal Commission on Labour in 1929 recommended that the "Government should take lead in case of their industrial employees in making recognition of union easy and encouraging them to secure recognition".

(*b*) Legislative action was not taken until 1943 for compulsory recognition of Trade Unions by employees, when the Indian Trade Unions (Amendment) Bill, 1943 was placed before the Central Legislative Assemble. But the Bill was opposed by the management. So it could not be passed. Three years later the Bill in revised form was introduced in 1946 in the Central Legislative Assemble. The Bill was referred to the Select Committee, which suggested some amendments. The Bill was passed in November 1947 and received the assent of the Governor General in December 1947. But the Trade Unions (Amendments) Act was never brought into force.

In 1950 Trade Unions Bill also incorporated provisions for recognition of Trade Unions. The Bill was moved in the legislature but it could not take the form of the Act.

(*c*) The International Labour Organisation by convention No. 87 on "Freedom of Association and Protection of the Right to organize" in 1948, stated that workers or employers shall have the right to establish, and subject only to the rules of the organization concerned, to join organization of their own choice without previous authorization. The convention also empowers the workers organization to frame their constitution to elect representatives and to organize their activities. To establish and join federation Article 8 of the convention requires that workers and employers and their respective organizations, shall respect the law of the land.

ILO Convention No. 98 concerning the right to organize and bargain collectively in 1949 confers protection to workers against acts of anti-union discrimination in respect of their employment. The protection is directed in respect of acts calculated to:

(*i*) Make the employment of a worker subject to the conditions that he shall not join a union or shall relinquish trade union membership.

(*ii*) Cause the dismissal of or otherwise prejudice a worker by reasons of union membership or because of his participation in union activities outside working hours.

(*iii*) After Independence the Labour policy during the first plan gave importance to the recognition of trade union. The second plan recommended that some statutory provision for security recognition does not exist at present. The third plan marked the shift in the policy of recognition of trade unions. It was stated on the plan that "the basis for recognition of unions, adjusted as part of the Code of Discipline will have the way for the growth of a strong and healthy trade unionism in the country. A union can claim recognition if it has continuing membership of at least 15 per cent of the workers in the establishment over a period of six months. If there are several unions in any industry or establishment, the union with the largest membership will be recognized there should be no change in its position for a period of two years, if it has been adhering to the Code of Discipline".

(*iv*) The National Commission on Labour in 1966 also recommended for statutory recognition of trade unions, however no legislative action was taken till 1978.

(*v*) Industrial Relation Bill, 1978 had the provision for recognition of Trade Union. Although the Bill was introduced in Lok Sabha in August 1978, it lapsed after the dissolution or Sixth Lok Sabha in August 1978.

(*vi*) The hospitals and other institutions (Settlement of Disputes) Bill 1982.

The bill contains provisions for the recognition of the trade unions. For the purpose of recognition a trade union must be registered under the Trade Unions Act and each of its office bearers should be a workman and the union must have the support of majority of workmen in the establishment. The representative of workmen on the Grievance Settlement Committee, Local Consultative Council and Consultative Council would be Nominee of recognized Trade Unions.

Law and Practice to Recognition of Trade Unions

There are two main aspects concerned with the problem of trade union recognition. First is the problem of Legal recognition while the second question relates to the recognition of union by the employer. The employers have to accept the union's right to bargain on behalf of employees.

A. ***Legal Recognition Problem:*** Regarding legal provisions of recognition of Trade Union, we may consider the following sources.

1.*Indian Constitution and Recognition of Trade Union:* A question is raise, "Is right to grant recognition to Trade Unions a fundamental right"? This question has to be answered in negative. Because under Article 19(1) (c) of the constitution the right to form association does not carry with it the concomitant right that the employees should recognize the association. Hence neither withdrawal of recognition of the union nor the discontinuance of recognition infringes the fundamental right granted under the constitution.

2. ***Legislative Measures:*** In several advanced countries such as the USA, Canada etc. where collective bargaining and voluntary arbitration has developed, statutory provisions have been made for determining representative character of trade unions.
3. ***Trade Unions (Amendment) Act, 1947:*** There is no central enactment governing recognition of trade unions in India. However the Trade Unions (Amendment) Act, 1947 has provided for recognition of trade unions.
   (*i*) By agreement.
   (*ii*) By order of the court on satisfying the conditions laid down in the Act. But the Act has not been enforced.

(*a*) Regarding determination of Representative Union, Section 28E of the Act empowers the Labour Court to grant recognition where registered union fails to get approval of the employer within a period of three months.

(*b*) The Act lays down certain conditions under section 35 (D) and 25 (E) to be fulfilled for setting recognition.

(*i*) That all its ordinary members are workmen employer in the same industry or industries closely allied or connected with one another.

(*ii*) That it's representative of all workmen employed by the employer in that industry or industries.

(*iii*) That its rules do not provide for the exclusive from the membership of any class of workmen.

(*iv*) That its rules provide for procedure for declaring strike.

(*v*) That its rules provide that a meeting of its executives shall be held at least once in every six months.

(*vi*) That is registered Trade Union and that it has compiled with all provisions of this act.

(*c*) Regarding the rights of recognized trade unions, the act provides that the recognized trade unions have been conferred the right to negotiate with employees regarding matters connected with employment, non-employment or the terms of employment or the conditions of labour if all or any of its members and the employer is under an obligation to receive and send replies to letters sent by the executives and grant interviews to them regarding such matter.

(*d*) Regarding withdrawal of Recognition of Trade Unions, The Trade Union (Amendment) Act, 1947 under section 28G. The registrar or the Employer is entitled to apply to the Labour Court in writing for withdrawal of the recognition on any one the following grounds.

(1) That the executives or the members of the union have committed any unfair practice set out in section 28J, within three months prior to the date of the application.

(2) That the trade union has failed to submit any returns referred to in section 28I.

(3) That the trade union has ceased to be representative of the workmen referred to in clause (b) of section 28 (D).

On receipt of the application, the Labour Court is required to serve a show cause notice in the prescribed manner on the trade union as to why its recognition should not be withdrawn. If the court is satisfied that trade union does not satisfy condition for granting recognition. It shall make an order declaring withdrawal of recognition.

(*e*) Re-recognition of trade unions is provided under section 28H of the Act that the registered trade union whose recognition has been withdrawn under subsection (3) of section 28G to make an application after six months from the withdrawal of recognition.

4. ***The Trade Union Bill, 1950:*** The Trade Union Bill was introduced in the Parliament in 1950 which was mainly a consolidated attempt with some new provisions. The bill also provided for recognition of trade union where application was made by more than one union. The union having the largest membership preference over others. The recognized union will be given of collecting subscription, holding meeting on employer's premises and of collective bargaining. The Labour Court empowered under the bill to order for recognition trade unions. However on account of severe opposition the bill could be passed and lapsed on the dissolution of the legislature.
5. ***State Legislation:*** Some State Governments have passed legislation on the recognition of trade unions. They may be discussed as follows:

(a) *The Maharashtra State:* The Maharashtra Recognition of Trade Unions and Prevention of unfair labour practice Act 1972 provides for recognition of trade union for smooth working of the collective bargaining process in certain undertakings. The Act states that:

(*i*) A trade union applying for recognition must be registered under the Trade Union Act, 1926.

(*ii*) Only registered unions can be recognised.

(*iii*) There should one union in one industry or undertaking or in more than one undertaking in a local area.

(*iv*) The recognized union becomes the sole bargaining agent and its recognition cannot be challenged within a period of two years of its registration as a recognized union.

(*v*) The unrecognized minority unions have two rights.

(*vi*) To meet and discuss with employer or his representative the grievances of individual member relating to discharge removal retrenchment supervision terminating service.

(*vii*) To appear on behalf of its members employed in the undertaking at any domestic or departmental enquiry held by employer.

(*viii*) A union can apply for registration as the recognized union for an undertaking to the industrial court, set up under the Act, if during the preceding period of six months it has not less than 30 per cent of the total number employees employed in that undertaking as its members.

(*ix*) There shall not at any time be more than one recognized union in the same undertaking.

Cancellation of Recognition of Union

The recognition of the union can be cancelled by the Industrial court under any one of the following circumstances:

(*i*) If it's was recognized by mistake, or fraud or misrepresentation or

(*ii*) If its membership for a continuous period of six months have fallen below the minimum prescribed or

(*iii*) If the union after recognition has failed to observe all the conditions specified under section 19 such as membership subscription will not be less than 50 praise per month, auditor will audit the accounts at least once in financial year end. The executive committee shall meet at intervals of not more than three months or

(*iv*) If the recognized union is not bring conducted bona fide in the interest of the employees but in the interest of the employer or

(*v*) If it has instigated, aided or assisted in the commencement continuation of a strike which is deemed to be illegal or (*vi*) If registration of the union under the Trade Union Act has been cancelled or

(*vii*) If any other union has been recognized in its place.

(*b*) *C.P. and Berar:* the C.P. and Berar Act, 1947 lays down certain conditions for recognition of unions, such as the union membership during preceding six months the date of application, should not be less than 15 and 20 per cent as the state Government may prescribe for that local area of the employees employed in the industry in that area.

(*f*) *Madhya Pradesh:* The Madhya Pradesh Industrial Relations Act, 1960 provides that a union for the purpose of recognition shall have not less than 25 per cent of the total number of employees employed in the industry in such local area.

6. ***Tribunal Response:*** The unions attempts to bring the question of its recognition by management within the purview of industrial dispute proved futile. The Industrial Tribunal has consistently rejected the unions claim for its recognition by the management on the grounds that specific remedy was provided in the trade unions (Amendment) Act, 1947 which was un-enforced.

7. ***Non-statutory Code of Discipline in Industry:*** In order to fill the lacuna in the central law the Indian labour conference in its Sixteenth session provided for recognition of trade unions. It laid down the following criteria for their recognition.

(*i*) Where there are many unions then a union claiming recognition should have been functioning for at least one year for registration. But if there is only one union then this condition would not apply.

(*ii*) The membership of the union should cover at least 15 per cent of the workers in establishment concerned. Membership will be counted only of those who had paid their subscription for at least three months during the period of six months immediately receding the reckoning.

(*iii*) A union may claim to be recognized as representative union for an industry in local area if it has membership of at least 25 per cent of the workers of that industry in that area.

(*iv*) When a union is recognized there should be no change in its position for a period of two years.

(*v*) A representative union for an industry in an area should have the right to represent the workers in all establishments in the industry.

(*vi*) Only unions, which observe the Code of Discipline would entitle to recognition.

This code has not been effectively implemented. However the Court may interfere under Article 226 of the contribution ever where the recognition granted by the employer under the non-statutory code of discipline is withdrawn on flimsy grounds or erroneous basis or in violation of the principles of natural justice.

In the absence of any statutory recognition of trade unions the question is whether a civil suit is maintainable on an action by a union under voluntary code of discipline. The court answered this issue as negative.

Rights of Recognized Trade Union under the Code of Discipline

The question of rights of recognized and unrecognized unions was discussed during 20th session of Indian labour conference held in August 1962. After lot of discussion it was decided to keep the issue of rights of unrecognized unions pending for future considerations. However it was agreed that the unions getting recognition under the code of discipline could enjoy the following rights.

1. To raise issue and enter into collective agreements with employers on general questions concerning the terms

of employment and conditions of service of workers in an establishment or, in case of representative union, in an industry in a local area.

2. To collect membership fee or subscriptions payable by members to the union within the premises of undertaking.
3. To put up on the notice board on the premises of the undertaking in which its members are employed and affix thereon notice relating to meetings of accounts of its income and expenditure and other announcements which are not abusive, indecent or inflammatory or subversive of discipline or otherwise contrary to the code.
4. For the purpose of prevention or settlement of an industrial dispute:
   (*a*) To hold discussions with the employees who are members of the union, at the suitable place which the premises of office or factory or establishment as mutually agreed upon.

   (*b*) To meet and discuss with the employer or any person appointed by him for the purpose, the grievances of its members employed in the undertaking.

   (*c*) To inspect by prior arrangement, in an undertaking, any place where any member of the union is employed.
5. To nominate its representatives on joint Management Councils and
6. To nominate its representatives on the grievances committee constituted under the Grievance procedure in an establishment.
7. To nominate its representative on non-statutory bipartite committee or production committees, welfare committees, canteen committees, house allotment committees etc. setup by management.

The rights referred to above would be without prejudice to the privileges being enjoyed by the recognized unions at present either by agreement or by usage.

8. ***Response to the National Commission on Labour:*** The Commission has recommended for compulsory recognition of trade unions by the employers under the Central Legislation in industrial undertakings employing one hundred or more workers and where capital invested is above the stipulated size. In order to claim recognition by the employer the union must have the total membership of 30 per cent of the plant or establishment. It is also recommended where recognition is sought by more that one union. The larger union should be recognized. The commission was in favour of recognition of industry wise union over plant or unit union.

While explaining the mode of determination of representative character the Commission suggested alternative method of verification and ballot. It suggested that the proposed industrial relations commission should be empowered to decide the representative character of union either by examining membership or holding an election through secret ballot of all employees. But this method also may lead to confusion and it may affect industrial peace and harmony. The Commission had proposed certain rights of recognized trade unions. Which were criticized by the AITUC and other organizations as inadequate.

9. ***Trade Unions and Industrial Disputes (Amendment) Bill 1988:*** The Bill aimed at providing for the constitution of Bargaining Council to negotiate and settle industrial disputes. Under Chapter II-D every employer is required to establish a bargaining council for his industrial establishment consisting of representatives of all trade unions having membership of workmen employed in the establishment. When

there are more than one union with members who are work men employed in an industrial establishment then the representation of all such unions and bargaining council shall be in proportion to the number of members in the establishment as determined by the Trade Unions Act, 1926. The Central Government may establish a bargaining council for industries in the basis of relative strength of the trade unions of workmen concerned.

The Central Government may establish the National Bargaining Council in consultation with state governments for a class industry or a group of central public undertaking where appropriate Government is State Government. The National Bargaining Council shall consist of representative of Central and State Government concerned employees and their unions and trade unions of workers being represented in proportion to their relative strength of membership as determined under the provisions of the Trade Unions Act, 1929.

Conclusion

At present there is no central legislation relating to the recognition of the trade union, which is urgently needed today. It should provide for compulsory recognition of trade unions. It will help in settlement of disputes and will make such settlement to last for longer time. It will also prevent the disputes that arise due to inter union rivalry. It will make adamant and arrogant employers to recognize the representative union for making collective bargaining effective. It may promote uniformity to standards for the unions seeking recognition from their management.

International Trade Unions

International Labour Organization (ILO)

The ILO was established in the year 1919 to place the various labour problems on a regular international basis. ILO was established as a forum for international understanding.

The ILO has influenced the growth of labour movements in the country.

The ILO has been attempting to promote worldwide respect for the freedom and the dignity of the working men and to create the conditions which that freedom and dignity can be fully and effectively enjoyed.

Role/Functions of ILO

These are as follows:

(*i*) To prepare the first draft of the International Labour standards.

(*ii*) To organize, compile reports and provide secretariat services for the international Labour Organization Conference.

(*iii*) To conduct and carry out technical co-operation projects.

(*iv*) To undertake research and enquires and publish the results to implement the operational programmes.

(*v*) To publish periodicals.

(*vi*) To prepare the documents on the items of the agenda of the conference.

(*vii*) To assist Governments in framing legislations on the basis of the decisions of the International Labour Conference.

(*viii*) To collect and distribute the information on international labour and special problems.

(*ix*) To bring out the publications dealing with industrial labour problems of international interests.

(*x*) To formulate international policies and programmes to promote basic human rights to improve working and living conditions of labour and enhance employment opportunities.

(*xi*) To act as a cleaning house of information of labour matters.

(*xii*) To create intentional labour standards.

Fundamental Principles of ILO

These are as follows:

(*i*) Universal peace can only be established if it is based upon social justice.

(*ii*) Protection of children, young persons and women, protection of the interest of the migrant workers.

(*iii*) Recognition of the principles of freedom of association.

(*iv*) Organization of vocational and technical education.

(*v*) Improvement in the working conditions of the workers by regulating the work hours, provision of adequate living wages, protection of workers against sickness, diseases etc.

All the above principles of ILO are set out in the preamble to its constitution.

Structure of ILO

ILO is composed of three principal organizations, *i.e.* (*i*) International Labour conference; (*ii*) Governing Body; and (*iii*) International Labour office.

The conference is the supreme policy making and legislative wing. The Governing Body is the executive council and the international labour office is the secretariat for operational head quarters and information centre. It is located at Geneva.

The work of the conference and the governing body is supplemented by regional conferences and committees.

Changing Role of Trade Unions in Globalize Economic Environment

Trade Unions in India played a significant role in protecting the interest of the workers by controlling and regulating the management of the cost of the organization. But trade unions now play an important role by co-operating with the management as the survival of the organization under competitive environment would be at stake. Trade union's role fighting with the management in order to protect the interest of the workers would receive dismissal stake as most of the employment conditions would be determined by the market forces rather than by political and/or membership strength of trade unions. Further, the Government would support management rather than trade unions unlike in the past, as presently the Government's objective is to attain rapid economic development. Hence, the liberalization would not guarantee the same role and importance for the trade unions in India.

Trade unions in India resisted the implementation of economic liberalization as they do not generally favour multinationals getting free access into the Indian industrial field, do favour the growth small-scale sector, oppose privatization of public enterprises and do not want new economic policy on various platforms and through different means, have, in fact, not respond adequately to the possible fall-out in employment and salaries.

Role of Trade Unionism (Trade Union Movement) towards Child Labour

The ILO has adopted 13 conventions and 9 recommendations for the protection of children and young persons and promotion of their well being. ILO also has addressed the problems of child labour through programmes and projects at the national and local community level. The Modern Trade Union Movement in India has supported all this activities of I.L.O. significantly.

The Trade Union Movement in India also supported ILO's programmes called 'the International Programme on the Elimination of Child Labour' (IPEC).

The Trade Union movement in India also fights against the worst abuses of child labour, hazardous work, bonded child labours, forced child labour, the employment of working children who are less than 12 years of age.

Role of Indian Trade Union Movement for the Women Workers

The Indian Trade Union movement has made significant contributions in fighting against discriminatory practices against women workers. Indian trade union movement activities regarding this cause includes research, evaluation meeting, technical co-operation and dissemination of information.

The Indian trade union movement supported the I.L.O fight against unequal remuneration to the women workers, discrimination against employment and occupation.

The Indian trade union movement always fights against the cruel practices of night work, underground work regarding women. It also fought for the up-liftment of working conditions in respect of women.

Role of Trade Union Movement in Respect to Software Professional (Industries)

The growing unionism of software professionals (white-collar unionism) has become a predominant trend in India in recent decades.

The increasing number of software industries in India in recent past has give rise to software professionals unionism.

The trade union movement in respect of software professional has attributed the following benefits to them.

(*i*) Job guarantee and security;

(*ii*) Better pay packages;

(*iii*) Better working conditions;

(*iv*) Respectable and equal treatment from the employer.

Role of Trade Unionism with Respect to Casual and Badli Workers: It is as follows:

(*i*) To get the economic security to these workers.

(*ii*) To provide them with steady employment with adequate income.

(*iii*) To restrain the management from any illegal action against these workers.

(*iv*) To communicate the views, ideas, feelings and frustrations of these workers to the management.

(*v*) To secure these workers from economic hazards beyond their control.

(*vi*) To try to regularizes the employment of these workers by negotiating with the management.

Workers Federation of Trade Unions (W.F.T.U.)

This led to Paris Conference in Sept-Octo. 1945, which saw the official constitution of the World Federation Of Trade Unions – WFTU. This federation was hailed as a powerful instrument of peace and goodwill among mankind. The main objectives existed, along with others, were:

- To improve the living and working conditions of the people of all lands.
- To unite them in pursuit of the objectives sought by all freedom loving people.
- To plan and organise the education of trade union members on the question of international labour unity.
- To awaken them to a consciousness of their individual responsibility towards trade union purpose and aims.

At the time formation of the WFTU in 1945, was represented by 65 Mn. members. This membership increased to 108 Mn. in 1957 and 150 Mn. in 1965. From our country AITUC is affiliated to WFTU.

International Confederation of Free Trade Unions (ICFTU)

This however, did not last long due to the conflict between communist and non-communist groups. The non-communist labour organisations, therefore formed the "international confederation of free trade unions in Nov. 1949. This ICFTU stands for free and democratic trade unionism, independent of any external domination. It is pledged to the task of promoting the interests of working people throughout the world and enhancing the dignity of labour. Its objectives could be summed up in three words : "Bread, Peace and Freedom". Its functions are based on recognition of the fact that, "industrial and social problems of working people in all industries and countries have many things in common". It is interested in problems of economic planning, unemployment, industrial accidents and diseases and joint consultations etc. Between 1949-1962 the membership of ICFTU was grown up from 48 to 57 million. In 1965, it had 121 affiliated organisations in 96 countries with around 60 million members. From India, INTUC and HMS are affiliated to it. ICFTU also took special interest in organising training programmes for trade union education.

International Labour Organisation—ILO

On the background of all these development around the world, the "ILO—the International Labour Organisation", was formed. It is an inter-government institution having 123 countries as its members, including India who is also its member since inception in 1919. It is tripartite in character and representatives of governments, employer and labour organisations participate in its work. It has been functioning as a specialised agency of the United Nations since 1946.

The ILO aims at promoting social justice in all countries. It collects and disseminates information about labour and social conditions. It also formulate international standards and supervises their application by nation members. It is also engaged in operational activities and providing technical assistance in carrying out social and economic development programmes. It comprises of three principle organs, namely the General Conference, the Governing Body and the International Office. The conference adopts international labour standards, which the formulated in special international treaties called "Conventions and Recommendations". The international Labour Office is its permanent secretariat, with head quarters in Geneva. This office undertakes inquiries, research and publishes its results.

International Labour Organisation—Standards (ILO)

One of the most fundamental obligations imposed on governments by the constitution of the ILO is, that they must submit the instruments to the competent national authorities, which have the power to legislate or take other actions in order to give effect to "Conventions and Recommendations". ILO standards are considered both useful and capable of application, since as many as 136 conventions by some 123 countries have been registered in the past. While framing of the Conventions and Recommendations, the conference takes into consideration such factors as climatic conditions, industrial organisations and other special circumstances in different countries. It has for instance, inserted in certain Conventions, lower age standards for countries like India, Pakistan, China and Japan.

Flexible clauses of ILO, help in making the ILO standards applicable to the less industrialised countries. Conventions and Recommendations by the member countries, are termed in International Instruments. Thus Conventions and Recommendations taken together are known as the "International Labour Code". The standards adopted covered all sorts of matters, such as freedom of association, conditions of work, protection to women and young workers, labour management relations, safety and hygiene, social security, and therefore these have good impact over the daily life of every worker. However, if any member country finds it difficult to ratify any of the conventions through laws, it must send a report indicating the difficulties faced by it and modification being thought.

If the standards have to show any real and permanent meaning, these must be converted into laws and practices by that country, which accepts them. The ILO has a set procedure to ensure that the promise is matched by performance. The Director General [exe. Head] submits annual report on the application of ratified conventions, to the annual conference.

CHAPTER

3

Industrial Disputes

Characteristics of Industrial Disputes

For a dispute to become an industrial dispute, it must satisfy the following conditions:

(1) There must be a dispute or a difference

(*a*) Between employers and employees

(*b*) Between employers and workmen or

(*c*) Between workmen and workmen.

(2) A dispute should be connected with the employment or non-employment or the terms of employment or with the conditions of labour of any person or it must be relating to any industrial matter.

(3) A workmen does not draw any wages more than Rs. 1600 per month.

(4) The relationship between the employer and workmen should be in existence and should be a result of the contract and the workman actually employed.

The term industrial dispute has been interpreted and analyzed differently in cases by the courts. Some of the principles to judge the nature of dispute evolved by the courts are as follows:

(*i*) The dispute must affect large group of workmen who have community of interests and the rights of these workmen must be affected as a class in the interest of common good.

(*ii*) The dispute should invariably taken up by the industry union or by an appreciable number of workmen.

(*iii*) There must be a concerned demand by the workers or redress and the grievance becomes such that it turns from industrial complaint into general complaint.

(*iv*) The parties to the dispute must have direct and substantial interest in the dispute, *i.e.* there must be same nexus between the union which exposes the cause of the workmen and the dispute. Moreover, the union must fairly claim a representative character.

(*v*) If the dispute was in its inception, an individual dispute and continued to be such still the date of its reference by the government for adjudication, it could not be converted into an industrial dispute by support subsequent to the reference even of workmen interested in the dispute.

By incorporating section 2A in the Industrial Disputes Act, 1947, a right has been given to the industrial worker himself to raise an industrial dispute with regard to termination, discharge, dismissal or retrenchment of his service even though no other workman nor any trade unions of workers raised it or is a party to dispute.

Industrial unrest takes organized form when the work people make common cause for their grievances against employers through manifestations of strikes, demonstrations, picketing, morchas, gheraos, gate meetings etc.

Industrial Conflicts Vs. Disputes

The term industrial conflict is rather a general concept, but when it acquires specific dimensions, it is known as industrial disputes.

Although the term conflict is usually viewed negatively as undesirable and dysfunctional, there are some respects in which conflict is functional to groups and also to individuals.

Kornhauser and others have stated the main functions of inter-group conflict as follows:

(*i*) Conflict provides stability to the group concerned. For example: Workers show greater unity during the period of crisis while management shows greater homogeneity during a period of strikes.

(*ii*) A situation of conflict helps and forces the groups to bring out the issues of different in open so that is becomes easier to overcome them.

(*iii*) When conflicts are made open, the groups involved get public attention and they have to subject themselves to public opinion.

(*iv*) During periods of conflict, groups, tend to bring out all the powers at their command. Even within a group, activities and decisions tend to rest with the persons who wield maximum power. Thus conflict helps in identifying power centers in and between groups.

Although the conflicts are functional to certain extent, still open conflicts in the form of strikes, lockouts etc. are certainly dysfunctional and undesirable. So conflicts need to be managed effectively.

The term industrial dispute is used to denote work stoppages and those differences between labour and the management that are settled through the industrial relations machinery.

When the issues of conflict are submitted to the management for negotiations, they take the form of industrial disputes.

Features of Industrial Conflicts in India

According to Mamoria and others, the main features of industrial conflicts are as follows:

1. Many of the present day conflicts are not concerned with cost benefit consciousness on the part of the labour.

Many of them were long drawn out. The issue raised by the strikes and the quantitative benefits even in the cases of total success, show a lack of proportion to the disadvantage of labour, it is as though damage and loss to the employer rather benefits for labour have been the objectives of the struggle.

2. Another trend is the frequency with which management met, "Labour pressure by the management pressure of lockouts".
3. Most of the strikes are political strikes *i.e.* they are not caused by any industrial disputes as such. Among these are included physical restraint such as bundhs, gheraos, dharana etc. go slow and work to rule. All these practices indicate that the dimensions of conflict in industrial relations are growing and cause significant loss of mandays. A single day's bandh cause a loss of one million mandays in advanced states of India.
4. Similarly, on account of lockouts, several mandays are lost. Such lockouts are common in eastern region. The average duration of lockouts is longer than the strikes, because lockouts represent employer's resistence and in India, employers has more resources to ride out a period of stoppages.

Modern Trends in Industrial Conflicts

Since independence, Indian government has taken several steps to promote industrialization at a higher rate and skill formation and welfare of the working class. As a result, now the migrant nature of the labour has disappeared and they have become urban skilled and stable labour force.

Indian social structure has been transformed significantly as a result of the modernization of the economy characterized by technological progress, organizational complexity and increasing inter-dependence. As a result, the status of the worker has improved from a simple commodity to creative and self managing entity.

Secondly, need for taking quick decisions has increased because of high stakes that are involved in modern technologically advanced capital intensive processes adopted by the big organizations. Several public sector units are being managed by the bureaucratic rather then professional managers, hence decision-making process is delayed leading to crisis. There is an urgent need to remove all these shortcomings in order to avoid disputes and to maintain healthy industrial relations.

It may be noted that the present Industrial Disputes Act, 1947 has been based on sections 81 and 81 of the defence of India rules framed by the British government for India to manage industries during war item. In the act to the emergency provisions was added compulsory adjudication and third-party or government intervention. Thus, the entire process has become politicized. So, according to Mamoria and others, "Unless these provisions of the defence of India rules are removed, there will be no lasting solution of industrial unrest. It is obvious that the machinery of industrial relations should tackle disputes within the framework and the spirit of a dynamic bi-partite approach like husband and wife solving their problems themselves within the framework of the marriage".

Types of Disputes

Mamoria and others have classified the industrial disputes as follows:

(*i*) On the basis of terms of employment.

(*a*) Interest disputes or economic disputes

(*b*) Grievance or rights disputes

(*ii*) On the basis of organizational rights.

(*c*) Disputes over unfair labour practices

(*d*) Recognition disputes

(*iii*) According to the nature of conflict.

(*e*) Strikes

(*f*) Lockouts

Let us discuss them in details:

(a) Interest Disputes or Economic Disputes

These are the conflicts that arise about the issues in which economics interests of the workers are involved such as revision in wages, fringe benefits, job security and other conditions related to employment. In the absence of mutually binding standards for settlement of interest disputes, it ultimately depends upon the bargaining power of the parties, compromise, economic strength of the parties that enable to arrive at an agreed solution. As these issues are subject to compromise, it depends upon give and take process and the bargaining skills between the parties.

(b) Grievances or Rights Disputes

These are also known as conflicts of rights or legal disputes. These conflicts arise from day to day working relations in the organization as the protests against certain acts or decisions of the management, which are considered as violating the rights of the employees. These conflicts arise on the issues relating to discipline, transfers, dismissal, payment of wages and other fringe benefits like working hours, overtime, promotions, demotions, rights of supervisions and union leaders safety and health provisions, interpretation and application of collective agreements. Hence, they are known as interpretation disputes. As there is no definite standard for settling a grievance of dispute available, it depends on the relevant provision of the collective agreement, employment contract, work rules, customs, laws etc voluntary arbitration is encouraged by the government for settlement of this type of disputes.

(c) Disputes over Unfair Labour Practices

Many times, management may discriminate workers because they are the active members of the trade union or they are participating in union activities, especially those employees who are union officials or those participating in strikes. Secondly, management may create obstacles of several types in the process of formation of union, or exercise their right to organize, join or assist the union, establishing employer-sponsored unions, refusal to bargain collectively with organized union, recruiting new employees during legal strikes, unwillingness to implement award etc. such disputes are settled according to the procedure laid down under the Industrial Disputes Act.

(d) Recognition Disputes

When the management refuses to recognize a trade union for the purpose of negotiations and collective bargaining recognition disputes come into existence of management attitude, as in case of victimization, the management may refuse recognition on the grounds of non-representative character of the union, multiplicity of union claiming for recognition. In such cases, the conflict may be resolved with the help of the rules made by the organizations for the recognition of unions for collective bargaining. These rules may not be laid down by law, but maybe conventional or customary in nature. In some countries, such rules are covered by voluntary codes of discipline or industrial relations characters accepted by both the parties.

(e) Strikes

Generally, the strikes are results of fundamental maladjustments, injustices and economic disorders. Industrial Disputes Act, 1947 under section 2(q) defines strike as a cessation of work by a body of persons employed in any industry, acting in combination or concerted refusal under a common understanding, of a number of persons who are or have been so employed to continue to work or to accept employment.

According to Peterson, "strike is a temporary cessation of work by a group of employees in order to express grievances or to enforce a demand concerning changes in work conditions".

Thus, strike possesses three main elements which are: (*i*) plurality of workmen; (*ii*) cessation or refusal to work by the employees; and (*iii*) combined or concerted action by the workmen for the purpose of enforcing a demand, and it must be in defiance of the authority of the employers.

Strikes may be classified in different ways.

(1) They are Classified in four ways:

1. ***Economic strike:*** Employers and employees have a duty to negotiate in good faith. Good faith may be breached by: (*i*) refusing to respond to a party's request to bargain; (*ii*) Refusing to send bargaining representatives for negotiations without sufficient authorit; (*iii*) Continuously shifting bargaining position to obstruct the conclusion (*iv*) Campaigning to undermine bargaining representatives; (*v*) Refusing to make counter proposal at all. Thus if the parties have negotiated in good faith but fail to reach an agreement, a strike that follows contract expiration is called economic strikes.
2. ***Unfair labour practice strikes:*** If a strike is provoked or prolonged by an employer's unfair labour practice, then employers are held guilty of causing unfair labour practice strike.
3. ***Wild cat strikes:*** A wild cat strike occurs in violation of collective bargaining agreement without official approval of union leaders.
4. ***Illegal strike:*** Strikes which are declared illegal according to the provisions of the industrial disputes act are illegal strikes.

(2) Three-way Classification of strikes

According to this method, strikes are classified as primary strikes, secondary strikes and other strikes.

I. ***Primary Strikes:*** These strikes are against the employer with whom the dispute has taken place. Primary strike may take any form as discussed below:

   (i) *Stay-away strike:* When the workers stay away from the workplace and organize rallies, demonstrations etc. stay-away strike takes place.

   (ii) *Stay in or sit-down strike:* In this type of strike, workmen come to the workplace, they are present at workplace but they do not work.

   (iii) *Tools-down-pen down-mouth shut strike:* When the strikes lay down their tools in case of factory workers and office workers lay down their pens and teachers shut down their mouths, then tool down strike comes into existence.

   (iv) *Token or protest strike:* This is a strike of very short duration and is a signal of the danger in future. Here workers may not work for an hour or a day only.

   (v) *Lightening or wild-cat strike:* Where the employees go no strike without any prior notice or with very short notice.

   (vi) *Go slow strike:* In this strike, workers work at a very slow speed as compared to normal speed of work.

   (vii) *Work to rule or work to designation:* When the workers decide to work according to rules or job description, this type of strike takes place.

   (viii) *Picketing and boycott:* It includes the act of posting pickets and patrolling of the workers in front of premises of the employer and to prevent other from entering the place. Boycott is an appeal for voluntary withdrawal of co-operation, to disrupt normal working of the unit.

(ix) *Gherao:* It is a physical blockade of the employer, manager or their representative by encirclement to block movement or the regress or ingress from and to a particular place in the organization.

(x) *Hunger strike:* This strike is adopted either by the union leaders or some workers all at a time or in small batches for a limited period of for a period till settlement of disputes takes place.

***II. Secondary Strikes*:** These are the strikes leveled against third party. They are also called as sympathetic strikes.

III. Other Strikes: These strikes cover general, particular, political and bandhs types of strikes.

(f) Lock-outs

According to Industrial Disputes Act, 1947, lock-outs means the closing of a place of business of employment or the suspension of work or the refusal by the employer to continue to employ any number of persons employed by him.

Thus lock-out is the action of an employer resulting into temporary closing down his production unit or refusing to provide his workers with work. The intention to force them to accept his demands or to withdraw demands of the employees made to him.

Features of Lock-out

1. Lock-out is the closure of industrial unit by the employer on account of existence or apprehension of an industrial disputes or violence and loss of properties.
2. It is a suspension employment relationship.
3. It is a counterpart of strike. As employees have the weapon of strike to put pressure on the employer, the employer may use the weapon of lock-out to bring pressure on employees to accept his terms and conditions.

4. Lockout is considered as an overt act of the employers with motive of ill-will.

However the following acts are not lock-out:

(*a*) Prohibiting an individual employee is not lock-out.

(*b*) Termination of employment by retrenchment is not a lock-out.

(*c*) Termination of services of more than one employee at the same time would not amount to lock-out.

(*d*) Declaration of lockout by an employer merely because workers have refrained from attending the work.

Thus, strikes and lock-outs both are harmful to the employees and employer, as well as the society. Hence, these need to be avoided as far as possible.

Various Reasons/Causes of Industrial Disputes in India

According to Leste, "when people sell their services and spend their working lives on the premises of the purchaser of those services, a varying amount of dissatisfaction, discontent and industrial unrest are likely to occur. The employees are specially interested in higher wages, healthy working conditions, opportunity to advance, satisfying work, some voice in industrial affairs and protection against loss of wages, overwork and arbitrary treatment. But when such things are denied to them, (because employers cut down their expenditure on labour to increase their own profits), they are forced to exert their rights to stop working to make the employers understand their grievances and redress them".

Industrial relations may be healthy or strained. The causes of strained relations are many that are rooted in historical, political, social, economic, cultural, psychological etc. factors, as well as the attitudes of the workers and employer. Industrial conflicts and disputes arise on account of several reasons. So they knew as multidimensional, dynamic and complex phenomena. A large variety of causes resulting into industrial disputes may be summarized as follows:

A. Management Related Causes

(*i*) Lack of proper policy of union recognition as bargaining agents on behalf of their members.

(*ii*) No delegation of proper authority to the recognized union.

(*iii*) Neglect of human relations while behaving with workers.

(*iv*) Lack of proper communication with employees.

(*v*) Practices of undeserved punishments, mass discharges, assaults, abuses, mischief's, victimization and maltreatment of workers of union, unfair labour practices.

(*vi*) Attitude of hatred towards labour.

(*vii*) Defective policy of layoff.

(*viii*) Maltreatment and wrong penalization of workers.

(*ix*) Inadequate collective bargaining arrangements.

(*x*) Arbitrary wage cut policy and massive dismissals without giving any explanation.

(*xi*) Lack of proper, definite wage policy.

(*xii*) Denial of workers rights to unite.

(*xiii*) Promoting inter-union rivalry and bribing trade union leaders.

(*xiv*) To induce workers to industrial disputes.

(*xv*) Not respecting registered agreements, settlements or awards.

(*xvi*) Dispute on demarcation of functions of employees.

(*xvii*) Unwilling to discuss with employees or their leaders but entertaining third party intervention.

(*xviii*) Insisting on referring the matter to arbitration even when union leaders are ready to co-operate.

(*xix*) Belief that management alone is responsible for recruitment, selection, promotion, transfers etc.

(*xx*) Neglect of providing proper services and benefits to workers.

(*xxi*) Introducing modernization without taking workers in confidence and creating proper environment.

(*xxii*) Insistence on maximization of profits by minimizing labour costs.

(*xxiii*) Lack of competence among supervisory and other managerial staff in maintaining and promoting human relation.

(*xxiv*) Mental inertia and conservative attitude.

(*xxv*) Neglecting demands of workers relating to wage increase etc.

B. Union Related Causes

1. Small unions with unstable membership.
2. Multiplicity of unions.
3. Inter-union rivalries and intra-union conflicts.
4. Weaker financial position.
5. Weaker bargaining power.
6. Outsider leadership which may not be aware of labour problems but uses union selfish, political ends.
7. Inability of union to protect interests of workers.
8. Differences with management in sharing gains of productivity.
9. Union leaders supporting management during negotiations.
10. Functioning of unions on the basis of caste, language, communal consideration etc. which tend to divide workers rather than creating solidarity among them.
11. Lack of communication and close contact with management.
12. Agitation and propaganda by selfish labour leaders to further interests of their own party and using the union for selfish motives.

13. Inability of unions to assume their responsibilities properly.
14. Unhealthy inter-union and intra-union rivalry.
15. Instability of trade union, as most of the unions function like 'strike committees'.
16. Growing functional and personal differences among rank and file of labour.
17. Wrong leadership leading to the spirit of non-co-operation and apathy.
18. Tendency to criticize and oppose management policies and decisions eventhough they are in right direction.
19. Giving excessive emphasis on wages and related matters neglecting other aspects related to work of life of employees.
20. Political affiliation of trade unions is generally used to increase strength of political party at cost of interests of workers.
21. Party in power favours unions affiliated to it, giving rise to inter-union conflicts.
22. Neglect of intra group and inter-group problems.

C. Worker-related Causes

1. Inadequate wages and earnings leading to deterioration in the standard of living.
2. Instability in employment or the need for security being not satisfied.
3. Disagreeable working and living conditions.
4. Absence of opportunity for self-expressions.
5. Lack of communication and contact with management.
6. Neglect of discipline.
7. Issues relating to leave, hours of work etc. not solved over long time.
8. Mental inertia.

9. Desire to have more wages, higher bonus and D.A.; which is rejected by management.
10. Excessive work load.
11. Inadequate welfare facilities.
12. Tendency not to respect union leaders and management representatives, but respecting and supporting outsiders.
13. Increase in insubordination and disobedience among workers.
14. change in attitude and temperament of workers due to education, adoption of urban culture, congruent changes in social values, growth of public opinion, progressive legislation enacted for the benefits if workers which made them conscious of their rights and intolerance of injustice or wrong done to them.

D. Other Causes

1. Absence of adequate machinery for collective bargaining.
2. Sympathetic or political strikes for political reasons.
3. Adverse socio-economic and political environment affecting attitude of workers towards work and management.
4. Excessive legislation and legal complexities regarding preservation of industrial peace and settlement of industrial disputes.
5. Lack of necessary changes in the functioning of government machinery to suit changing needs and circumstances.
6. Compulsory adjudication has made trade unions redundant at wages and working conditions of industrial employees will be determined by the courts, Tribunals and Wage Boards instead of trade unions.
7. Poor and ineffective implementation of legislation relating to labour and industries.

8. Failure of legislation to meet the needs of time.
9. Legislation becoming irrelevant in the context of challenges of present climate.
10. Poor implementation of legislative provisions by employers.
11. Poor performance of conciliation machinery of the government.
12. Loss of confidence of both parties in conciliation procedures.
13. Tendency of labour and management to become more litigation minded.
14. Inadequacy of conciliation machinery to solve all the cases referred to it as faster rate.
15. Lack of training of conciliation officers in handling problems of disputes referred to them.
16. Political instability, poor enter-state relations etc.
17. Other political factors such as corruption, character crisis, breakdown of national morale, debasement of social value and industrial norms etc. may lead to industrial unrest, conflicts.

An industrial dispute are very costly for developing economies, every attempt should be made to prevent them and even if they arise, they should be immediately settled.

Effects of Industrial Disputes

The impact of industrial dispute is deep rooted having wider consequences. Because they disturb social, economic and political life of a country and may make economic planning ineffective.

As industrial dispute is like a stone thrown in a pond, causing a series of waves, affecting the pond as a whole. Thus, because of conflicts, not only employers ad employees, but also the consumers, community and the nation as a whole have to suffer very seriously.

Industrial disputes result into stoppage of work flow, leading to the huge wastage of mandays and installed capacity and dislocation of production work. A strike in public utility service like power or railways may affect public life making people to suffer severe hardships. Shortages of goods may result into inflationary conditions for difficult to control in time.

As a result of disputes, workers and their family members are seriously affected. Their regular income flow comes to an end and workers already living at near subsistence level have to raise debts, which they find it difficult to repay. When frustration among workers increases, they may become violent. So they may be prosecuted, victimized or beaten by goondas. Unsuccessful strikes are still worst. A weak trade union may become still weaker and may die permanently.

The employers also have to suffer heavy losses not only on account of work stoppages, but also, taking steps to settle the disputes legally or illegally. In addition, there is a loss of mental peace, respect and status in society. Which cannot be evaluated easily in terms of money.

As a result of industrial dispute, resulting into strikes and lock-outs, the society also suffers on account of shortages of essential goods and services. It also creates law and order problems and even if disputes are settled, still bitterness and strife may continue and strain social relations. The strikes and lock-outs affect the society just like war conditions affect it.

Industrial disputes also affect national economy by way of reduction in national income and making people poor with lower purchasing power, resulting into lower level of effective demands. As Prof. Pigou has observed, "When labour and equipment in the whole or any part of an industry are rendered idle by a strike or lock-outs, national dividend must suffer in a way that injures economic welfare. It may happen in two ways. On the one hand, by impoverishing the people actually involved in the stoppage, it lessens the demand for the goods, the other industries make it. On the other hand, if the industry in which the stoppage has occurred is one that finishes a commodity or service largely used in the conduct of other industries, it lessens the supply to them of raw material or equipment for that work. This results in a loss of output, ultimately reducing the national income". That in turn may affect developmental activities to be undertaken according to the plan priorities.

As Catlin has pointed out, "the strikes and lock-outs are a great menace to public safety. They infringe upon property rights and become malicious to public safety. They infringe upon property rights and become malicious in their effects, if not in their purpose and they are regarded as a war or at any rate a blockade".

The Industrial Disputes Act, 1947

After the end of the First World War around 1919, there was a great industrial unrest. However it took another few years for legislation, and the Trade Disputes Act was passed in 1929 by the Government of India. Thus we can say that the history regarding handling industrial disputes is not very old in our country. The Act empowered the Government to intervene the industrial dispute, whenever it thought to be appropriate. It contained special provisions for public utility services. Regarding strikes, because that affect the general life of the common man. This Act was amended in 1938 authorising the Central and Provincial Government to appoint the conciliation officers for mediating in conflicts or promoting the settlement of industrial disputes. But during the Second World War the situation became again delicate and the Government had to introducer DIR giving more powers to it for appointment of industrial tribunals. Thus, The Industrial Disputes Bill was introduced in the Central Legislative Assembly during October, 1946. The Bill was passed by the assembly and it became the law from 1st April, 1947.

This Act, as amended from time to time, became the beginning of industrial adjudication in India. It has so far been amended on 34 major and minor occasions by the Parliament, including the latest amendments in 1982 and 84. The Act has 9 chapters and 40 sections. The Objectives of this Act are:

Objectives

- To provide for the investigation and settlement of industrial disputes.
- To settle the disputes between the capital and labour by peaceful methods using machinery like conciliation, arbitration and tribunals.
- To prevent illegal strikes and lockouts.
- To provide compensation to workmen in lay off, retrenchments, and closures, there by protecting them against victimisation.
- To promote collective bargaining through which ensuring social justice to both employers and employees.
- To advance industrial progress by bringing about harmony and cordial relations between the parties.

While settlement of disputes, the question of appropriate Government needs to be seen in the cases where the entire business of an undertaking is limited to one state and the other case where the employer has establishments in more than one state. The Act does not contain any provision in this respect, nor it clearly states about joint reference by both state together. Courts had in the past taken the decisions as per the jurisdiction limits observed by the civil courts.

Definition of Industry

The term 'industry' has been defined under sec.2(j) as " any business, trade, undertaking, manufacture or calling of employees and includes any calling, service, employment, handicraft or industrial occupation or avocation of workmen". The definition is exhaustive and comprehensive in scope. It is in two parts. One part of it defines from the standpoint of the employer, the other part from the standpoint of the employee. The Supreme Court by a judgement of far reaching importance, delivered on 22-2-1978, gave a wide implication to the meaning of industry. It laid down a triple test to decide the application of the I.D. Act to them. The triple test is :

- Systematic Activity.
- Co-operation between employer and employees.
- Production and/or distribution of goods and services calculated to satisfy human wants and wishes.

If these tests are satisfied, then any activity is an 'industry'. The decisive test is functional and the focus is on the nature of the activity with special emphasis on the employee-employer relations. Absence of profit motive or gainful objective is irrelevant wherever the undertaking is - whether in the public, joint, private or other sector. All organised activities possessing the triple elements, although not trade or business, may still be industry provided the nature of the activity on the employee-employer basis bears resemblance to what is found in a trade or business.

This would take into the fold of the word 'industry' all undertakings, calling and services analogous to the carrying on the trade or business. Therefore clubs, professions, educational institutions, co-operatives, research institutes, charitable projects and others, if they fulfil the above triple tests, cannot be exempted from the scope of sec. 2(j). However, a restricted category of professions, clubs, co-operatives and even gurukuls and little research labs may qualify for exemption if, in simple ventures, substantially, and going by the dominant criterion, no employees are entertained but in minimal matters, marginal employees are hired without destroying the non-employee character of the unit. A single lawyer, a rural medical practitioner or urban doctor with a little assistance and/or menial servant may ply a profession but, may not be said to run an industry, because there is nothing like organised labour in such employment. Voluntary free medical clinic, Ashramites working at the building of the holiness etc., may be exempted. Where complex activities are carried on, the test will be what is 'dominant activity'.

Hospitals carry out systematic activities with organised co-operation between employer and employees, and also render the services to the human beings, hence hospitals are industries. The altruistic, charitable or non-profit intentions cannot be considered as basis for their exemption from defining them as industries. The term 'industry' must be analogous to trade or business and has an element of economic venture. Similar thinking is behind calling, schools, colleges, universities, solicitor's offices, gymkhana, clubs, institutes, charitable projects also within the definition of industry. The famous case of Tirupathi devasthanam is well known to all, where the employees working in water, electricity departments, and drivers, conductors etc. all formed a union and got it registered, because all these departments were working as industry and employees working, were workmen within the meaning of the Trade Union Act.

Industrial Disputes

Industrial dispute means "any dispute or difference between,

- Employers and employers,
- Employers and workmen,
- Workmen and workmen.

which is connected with the employment or non-employment or the terms of employment or with the conditions of labour or any person". The concept of employment involves employer-employee relationship and a contract of employment. An employer may dismiss a person or decline to employ him. This matter raises a dispute as a non-employment. Similarly, reinstatement is connected with non-employment. The definition of dispute is in three parts :

- Refers to the fact of real or substantial dispute,
- Parties to the disputes,
- Subject matter of the dispute.

Hence, unless a demand is raised by an employee and rejected by the management, there cannot be any industrial dispute. Such a dispute may be concerning a workman or a group of persons and raised by him or a group of persons, who has direct and substantial interest in the subject matter. Sometimes it could be an officer or other workman if there is a real community interest and this interest is direct immediate and non-remote. It is also said by the law that before any dispute between an employer and his workmen can be termed as an industrial dispute, it must be supported by a number of workmen. In other words, it is only a collective dispute that can constitute an industrial dispute. The person regarding whom the dispute is raised must be one in whose employment, non-employment, terms of employment or conditions of labour, the parties to the dispute have a direct or substantial interest.

Even a non-recognised and unregistered union may raise an industrial dispute, provided it is concerning substantial number of workmen who have a direct and substantial interest in the case. Even a minority union or minority group of workmen can raise an industrial dispute. If a discharged workman dies while contesting his termination his other fellow workers can raise this issue as an industrial dispute and his legal representative may continue his case in the Labour Court.

Conditions for Dispute

Recognition of union is a most important issue but recognition is not within the definition of 'industrial dispute' in the Act. It is not a condition of service or of employment or non-employment. An individual workman whose services are terminated can raise an industrial dispute and take his case to the conciliation machinery or approach the government for a reference of the dispute to adjudication. The object of the Sec. 2 is to give an industrial dispute relating to discharge, dismissal, retrenchment or otherwise termination, the status of an industrial dispute. When a dispute is sponsored by a trade union, and if its authority is challenged by the employer, it must be proved that the union has been duly authorised either by a resolution by its members or otherwise that the union has the authority to represent the workmen.

When an individual is covered under both the State and Central Act, he can raise a dispute under the State Act only. In the event if any member from the office bearers of a trade union withdraws himself from these duties, management may allow such a change as a concession but without any change in terms of service conditions. Hence this cannot be a subject matter of an industrial dispute under this section. To conclude, the following conditions must exist for an Industrial Dispute:

- There must be an industry.
- There must a relationship (workmen and employer) between the parties.
- The dispute must be connected with the employment or non-employment, terms of employment or the conditions of labour.
- The dispute must be related to a workman or any other person in whom, the group has a direct and substantial interest.
- The dispute should not be merely an industrial dispute, but should have some sense of a collective dispute.
- But in case of termination of services, an individual can raise an industrial dispute.

'Workman' means any person, including an apprentice, employed in any industry to do a skilled or unskilled, manual, supervisory, operational, technical or clerical work for hire or reward on the terms of employment expressed or implied. Unless a person is employed in an industry, he will not be a workman within the meaning of the definition. Similarly, a person who performs supervisory work and draws wages, exceeding Rs. 1600 p.m. is not a workman. There are four sub-clause of exception under Sec. 2 (S), under which if a workman is considered, he cannot be treated as a workman. A contractor is not a workman of Sec. 2(S). The same applied to the sub-contractor.

Persons employed by the employer and working as malis (gardeners) to look after the gardens attached to the bungalows of its officers or directors, which were situated within the mill colony of the employer, were treated as workmen. There are some accountants who are officers and some others who work as senior clerks, hence accountants working as clerks are in reality workmen only.

The question, whether a person is employed in a supervisory capacity or on clerical work, depends upon whether the main and principal duties carried out by him are of a supervisory character or of clerical in nature. If a person is doing mainly supervisory work, but on some occasions also works as a clerk, is a supervisor, and not a workman. The word 'supervisory' is not used in Sec. 2(S) in relation to the supervision of an automatic plant. The essence of 'supervisory' work is the supervision by one person over the work of the other persons.

To conclude, to determine whether a person is a workman or not, the mere title of the post held by him is not of much importance. What is to be seen is the nature of duties performed by him—nature of employment, main work performed, part of which is whether incidental or subsidiary etc. Definition of workman includes permanent and casual labourers both.

Special Features

Some special Features of the Act are:

(1) Works Committee

In a factory there are different kinds of people who differ in knowledge and skills, nature of their work, their attitude towards work and other people. With so many different people working together, misunderstandings, complaints and difficulties are likely to arise. If people can talk over these problems and try to solve them, things may workout smoother for the organisation.

Works Committee meetings provide opportunities for discussing these problems by its members and give them a chance to think and solve them, at the same time, if they can refer such things to the management and bring some changes.

(2) Purpose of Works Committee

Formation of Works Committees is provided under the Industrial Dispute Act, 1947. In this Act the purpose of the Works Committee is given as :

> "To promote measures for securing and preserving amity and good relations between the employer and the workmen".

In simple words, this means that the Works Committee should try to maintain good and friendly relations between both of them in the day to day working in the establishments. Following are some of the other major provisions regarding formation and functions of the Works Committees, as laid down under this Act:

Provisions and Functions

(1) Any employer who employs 100 or more workmen during preceding twelve months or at present, should constitute a Works Committee.

(2) The committee should consist of equal number of representatives from both the union and the management. All representatives should be the employees of the said establishment. The total number of members shall not be more than 20.

(3) All departments or sections should be represented by their members in the Committee, if possible.

(4) Workers' representatives elected to the Works Committee form two parts, one elected by the workmen-members of the registered trade union and the other who are not members of that union.

(5) The Chairman is nominated by the employer from amongst its representatives and the Vice Chairman is elected by the representatives of the workmen.

(6) The posts of The Secretary and the Joint Secretary are elected by the Committee, one each from the two groups comprising the Committee, and shall be elected every year, but shall not continue for two consecutive years.

(7) The Chairman and the Vice Chairman may hold office for not more than two consecutive terms.

(8) The representatives on the Committee shall hold the office for two years.

(9) The Committee may co-opt other persons with special knowledge in consultative capacity. They can be present only when such matter comes up for discussions, but they shall not have voting right.

(10) The Committee may meet as often as necessary, but at least once in three months.

(11) The employer shall provide accommodation to hold the meetings, which shall be conducted during working hours.

(12) The Government can dissolve the Works Committee, if it is not constituted as per the rules, if the meetings are not attended by its representatives on minimum number of occasions, or the Committee has stopped functioning.

(13) The Works Committee has to help to sort out the problems, by making its recommendations only, regarding the subjects like welfare of the employees,

recreation etc. to promote measures to preserve good relations between the employer and the workmen.

(14) The functions do not include to ascertain the grievances of the employees.

In 1959 the Indian Labour Conference set up a special committee, representing both employers and the trade unions, which drew up an illustrative list of subjects which Works Committee should normally deal with. The subjects include conditions of work, amenities like drinking water, canteen, dining rooms, safety and accident prevention, occupational diseases, adjustment of festival and national holidays, administration of welfare funds, educational and community development activities, measures on savings, implementation of the recommendations and decisions.

The special committee, however agreed that there should be some flexibility of approach and also that the demarcation would not be rigid.

In December 1966, the Government of India set up the National Commission of Labour (NCL) – to study the labour situation in the country and make necessary recommendations. The commission submitted its report in August, 1969 which states that the management should adopt more responsive attitude and extend whole hearted support in the implementation of the recommendations of the Works Committee. From the above observations it would be clear that both the employer and the trade unions, should take honest and sincere efforts to make Works Committee successful, by creating an atmosphere of trust on both sides. This shows that the Works Committee has to work with full support and co-operation of the union. In fact it should relieve the burden of the trade union as far as day to day problems in the factory are concerned.

Board of Conciliation

There is provision for the appropriate government to appoint a Board of Conciliation for promoting the settlement of any industrial dispute. This Board shall consist of the chairman and two to four members selected to represent both the parties. The chairman shall function as an independent person. If any of these parties fail to submit any recommendation within the prescribed time limit, the government appoints any suitable person to represent that party. The members of this Board enjoy more power than those enjoyed by Conciliation Officers. The Board has no own jurisdiction to admit any dispute, unless a reference is made to it by the government.

Industrial Tribunals

The Government may, by notification in the official gazette, constitute one or more industry tribunals for the adjudication of industrial disputes relating to any matter, as enlisted in the specified schedules of the Act.

National Tribunals

The Central Government may, by notification in the official gazette, constitute one or more National Tribunals for the adjudication of industrial disputes which in the opinion of the Central Government involve questions of national importance or, are likely to affect, or are of such a nature of one person by the Central Government. Since these are created by the government, they derive power from it only. They are not civil courts, but are courts of social justice. These have no inherent powers to decide any of the disputes raised by any of the parties. Such tribunals constituted under the Industrial Disputes Act, 1947 are only ad hoc tribunals to adjudicate upon a particular case referred to it, hence these are permanent tribunals.

Notice of Change

Sec. 9A was inserted and came into effect from March, 1957. Under this provision any "change in the conditions of service relating to wages, contribution to provident fund, hours of work and rest intervals, compensatory and other allowances, leave with wages and holidays, introduction of new rules of discipline, withdrawal of any customary concession or privilege" the employer should give 21 days' notice to all workmen, who are likely to be affected with such a change. No such notice is necessary if the changes are introduced out of any settlement or award. Any change can be introduced as per the procedure specified by the Act, which includes three stages like:

(1) The proposal by the employer to effect a change;

(2) The notice period given by him;

(3) Introduce change after the expiry of the notice period, from the date of notice. This provision safeguards the interests of the employees.

Voluntary Reference to Arbitration

Sec. 10-A was inserted and came into effect from March, 1957 which provides for the voluntary arbitration of industrial disputes. The employer and the workmen agree, by written agreement, to refer the dispute to arbitration, at any time before the dispute has been referred to a Labour Court or Tribunal. The agreement provides for the appointment of another person as an umpire. When the arbitrators are divided in their opinion, over the issue, the award of the umpire shall prevail and the same shall be deemed to be the award by the arbitration.

Powers of Labour Court and Tribunal

Every conciliation Officer, member of a Board, Court or Tribunal is deemed to be a public servant and may for the purpose of inquiry into any existing or apprehended dispute, enter the premises occupied by any establishment to which the dispute relates, after giving a reasonable notice. They exercise all the powers of a Civil Court while trying a suit. Every enquiry or investigation by a Board, Court or Tribunal shall be deemed to be judicial proceedings.

The conciliation Officer has been vested with the power to enforce attendance of any person for the purpose of examination of such a person.

The duties of the Board of Conciliation are similar to those of the Conciliation Officers. The time limit for submission of its report is two months, which can however be extended from time to time for further period, as may be agreed upon in writing by all the parties to the dispute. In case an industrial dispute has been referred to a Labour Court, Tribunal or National Tribunal for adjudication, it shall hold its proceedings and submit its award of a Tribunal must be in writing and the same must be signed by all its members.

The award of a Labour Court, Tribunal or National Tribunal must be signed by its presiding officer. Such report must be published within one month from the date of receipt of the report, by the appropriate government.

Where a Labour Court of Tribunal by its award directs reinstatement of any workman, but instead, the employer prefers to proceed against such award, in a High Court or Supreme Court, the employer is liable to pay full wages last drawn, including any maintenance allowance admissible, to such a workman, during the period of pendency of proceedings.

The legal position of a Labour Court or Tribunal while deciding a dispute arising out of dismissal or discharge of a workman was considered by the Supreme Court and certain power are given covering the areas, such as :

1. To satisfy itself, whether the employer has conducted a proper inquiry in accordance with the provisions of the standing orders and principles of natural justice, if an inquiry is not conducted by the employer the

Tribunal can satisfy itself by asking the employer to produce any evidences justifying the action, and similar evidence by the employee if needed. A case of conducting a defective inquiry stands on the same footing as no enquiry.

2. Right to grant a permission to such employee to produce any evidence for the first time before the Tribunal.
3. Right to interfere and decide the quantum of punishment, and the action of the employer is justified.
4. Punishment imposed by the employer cannot be interfered by the Tribunal, except in case of harsh punishment or victimisation.
5. Sec. 11-A was inserted in the Act and was brought into effect in December, 1971 which gave power to Tribunal, for the first time, to satisfy itself whether the misconduct recorded in the domestic enquiry is proved.

However, this section does not cover cases of retrenchment or retirement, because it clearly indicates that it is for discharge and dismissal cases only.

Settlements and Awards

Settlement is defined in Sec. 2(p) of the Industrial Disputes Act in two categories :

(*a*) One which is arrived at in the course of conciliation proceedings, with the assistance of Conciliation Officer.

(*b*) An agreement arrived at other than conciliation proceedings, between the employer and the workmen [this agreement should be in writing and signed by the parties, and copies sent to the officer authorised.] There is no restriction in the Act, on a private settlement between the parties even during the course of legal proceedings.

A settlement arrived at in the course of conciliation proceedings is binding for a period agreed upon by the parties. If no such period is mentioned, the settlement will remain in force for a period of six months from the date signing of it. The same will continue for a period of two months from the date on which one of the parties gives a notice to the other party its intention to terminate it.

There are certain principles laid down regarding settlements. These are :

1. Numerical strength of the members of the union which is the party to the settlement has an important bearing as to whether the settlement is accepted by the majority of the workmen.
2. A settlement reached in the course of collective bargaining is entitled to due weight and consideration.
3. The settlement has to be considered in the light of the conditions that were in force at the time of the settlement.
4. The principle of give and take during the negotiations is to be encouraged in the interests of general peace and well being.
5. The settlement has to be taken as a package deal and when labour gained in the matter of wages and if there is some reduction in dearness allowance, it cannot be said that the settlement as a whole is unfair and unjust. The package deal has to be accepted or rejected as a whole.
6. The question as to whether or not a settlement is just and fair is not to be decided by applying the principles of adjudication.
7. Acceptance of the fact that there may be several factors that may influence the parties to come to a settlement as a phased endeavour in the course of collective bargaining.

8. A settlement should not be highly and grossly unjust.
9. A settlement should not be seen in pieces and therefore some parts are held as bad and some others as good and acceptable.
10. The settlement signed by the large majority of the workmen holds good even if the same is challenged by the minority workmen.

By a settlement, the labour may scale down its claim and score in some other aspects and save unnecessary expenses in certain litigation. Once cordiality is established between the employer and the labour in arriving at a settlement which operates for a stipulated period, there is always a likely hood of further improved emoluments by voluntary settlement avoiding friction and unhealthy litigation. It is in this spirit the settlement on the expiry of the agreed period and to start the negotiations immediately thereafter.

The only condition is the fulfillment of two months' notice period ending on the expiry of the settlement and not before that. If the notice is given much in advance, and thus the notice period expires before this two months, the notice shall have no effect and the binding effect shall continue.

Validity of Award

An award is binding and will come into operation on the expiry of thirty days from the date of its publication and shall remain in operation for a period of one year from the date of its enforcement. However the appropriate Government may reduce this period, or extend the same by one more year, maximum up to three years only, if thought it as proper. Sometimes the government on its own or at the request of one of the parties, considers about a material change in the circumstances on which the award was based. Hence it may refer the award or a part of it to the Labour Court, Tribunal or National Tribunal for its decision whether the period of operation be reduce don the grounds of such a change. The decision given by these bodies becomes the final. Even when the stipulated period of operation expires, it shall be binding on both the parties up to two months from the date.

There is a difference between enforceability of an award and its coming into operation. The date of enforceability of the award of the tribunal is, the date of its publication. For any reason if the award does not become enforceable, it can never come into operation. However, the Tribunal has powers to indicate the date on which an award shall come into operation. When the tribunal directs grant of benefits from a specific date, then the award comes into operation from that date.

Strikes and Lockouts

The definition given under Sec. 2(q) state that, "Strike means a cessation of work by body of persons employed in any industry acting in combination, or a concerted refusal, or a refusal under a common understanding, of any number of persons who are or have been so employed to continue to work or to accept employment".

The condition of strike assumes certainly the plurality of workmen and refusal to continue to work by a group or any number of workmen. However, there are certain prohibitions of strikes that, in the following situations, workmen cannot resort to strike:

- When the conciliation is on before the Board of Conciliation.
- When arbitration is on before the Labour Court.
- When arbitration is on before the arbitrator.
- When a settlement or award is in operation.
- When and if an appropriate Government in its reference prohibits it.

Additional restrictions on strikes in public utility services are also elaborated under Sec. 22. The employers 'right to lockout is subjected to the same restrictions as the workmen' right to strike. The same rules apply with the same additional restrictions for public utilities. A strike is not illegal when it is declared because of an illegal lockout. There may be no special contract by the employees that they would not go on strike but still a strike by them may constitute a strike in breach of contract within the meaning of Sec. 22 and Sec. 23. The expression "breach of contract" in these two sections means only the contract of services or employment, either express or implied, of which a special contract not to go on strike is not an essential part.

In order to show that a strike is in breach of contract, it is not necessary to refer to any provision in the standing orders, which amount to a contract by the employees not to go on strike. But at the same time, some evidence must be produced against the breach of contract that the workmen were bound to come and work in the company and they did not. A strike is legal if it does not violate any provisions of the statute. Similarly, a strike cannot be said to be unjustified, unless the reasons for it are entirely unreasonable. Whether a particular strike is justified or not is a question of fact, which has to be judged in the light of the facts and circumstances of each case.

It is also well known that the use of force or violence or sabotage resorted to by the workmen during a strike does not entitle them to wages for the period of strike. Whether the strike is legal or illegal, the workmen are liable to lose wage for the period of strike. During the period of strike, the contract of employment continues, but if the workmen do not put in their labour, they cannot expect to be paid for the duration. The employer is not liable to pay either full days' salary or even a part of it, for the hours of work, because the employees remained in the work place without doing any work. Mere presence of the employees at the place of work is not sufficient, but the work they do according to the terms of contract, for which they are entitled to pay.

A lockout cannot be declared by an employer merely on the ground that the workmen have refrained from attending to work. If the strike resorted to by the workmen is found to be illegal, the workmen will not be entitled to salary or wages during the period of strike and it will not enable the employer to declare a lockout. The employer can declare a lockout only when he apprehends violence and loss to his properties. One has to know about the atmosphere on that particular day or a day before, to find out whether the lockout declared is justified or not. Whether there has been a voluntary abandonment of service or not is a question of fact which has to be determined in the light of the surrounding circumstances of each case.

The distinction between a 'lockout' and 'closure' has also been explained. In the case of 'closure' the employer does not merely close down the place of the business but he closes the business itself finally. In case of a lockout, it indicates the closure of the place of business and not the closure of the business. Lockout is used by the employer as a 'weapon' of collective bargaining, where as the closure is a matter of 'policy' of the employer whether to continue his business or not. If the undertaking is closed down, every workman who has been in continuous service for one year in that undertaking, shall be entitled to a notice and the compensation as done in case of a retrenchment.

Lay off and Retrenchment

Lay off

Sec. 2(kk) of the Act defines lay off as "the failure, refusal or inability of an employer on account of shortage of raw materials, power supply or sales orders (demand for its products), accumulation of stocks (finished goods or raw materials), break downs of machinery or any other reason to give employment to its workmen whose names are on the muster rolls of the industrial undertaking, but they have not been retrenched".

Provisions for lay off are applicable to those factories covered under Sec. 2(m) of the Factories Act, 1948 wherein 50 or more workmen on an average per working day have been employed in the preceding calendar month and which are not of seasonal character. In industrial undertakings where lay off provisions apply, only those workmen shall be entitled to lay off compensation whose names are on the muster rolls of the establishment, and who are not casual workmen, and have completed one year of continuous service with the said employer. The workmen shall be entitled for fifty per cent of the total basic wages and dearness allowances, as compensation, for all days in a week, except for the weekly holiday. No such compensation shall be paid to a workman,

(*a*) If he refuses to accept any alternative employment, on the same wages as in the previous job, in the same establishment belonging to the same employer, situated in the same town or village or a place situated within a radius of five miles from the establishment.

(*b*) If such lay off is due to a strike or slowing down of production on the part of a workman in another part of the establishment.

Retrenchment

Sec. 2(oo) defines retrenchment as " the termination of services of a workman by the employer for any reason other than a punishment imposed by way of disciplinary action". Voluntary retirement, superannuation, termination of employment on grounds of ill health do not amount to retrenchment. Workman who has completed one year can be retrenched if, he has been given one month's notice in writing indicating the reason for retrenchment or has been paid in lieu of such notice, and the compensation equivalent to fifteen days' average pay for every year of his completed service. Similar notice in the prescribed manner also needs to be given to the appropriate Government.

Transfer of Undertaking

Where the ownership or management of an undertaking is transferred to a new employer, every workman who has been in continuous service for one year in that undertaking before such transfer, shall be entitled to a notice and compensation as done in case of retrenchment. However such a notice and the compensation is not necessary if, his services have not been interrupted, the terms and conditions of the services are the same as before the transfer.

The Act was amended in March, 1976 imposing some restrictions on the employer's right to lay off, retrenchment and closure. These special provisions shall apply to all industrial establishments (except seasonal), in which not less than 300 workmen were employed on an average per working day for the preceding 12 months. Now this limit of employees is brought down to 100 with an amendment in 1984.

These three subjects are dealt separately in two chapters-VA and VB in this Act, on account of difference in reasons for lay off and retrenchment, taking into consideration the genuine power cuts and/or natural calamity etc. There are other sections which deal with the offences under this Act, committed by a company or a corporate body etc., committed by its employees in the categories like officers or the managers or its directors.

CHAPTER

4

Collective Bargaining

Features

Industrial peace and harmony is essential for economic progress of a nation. The concept of industrial harmony implies the existence of proper understanding, co-operation and a sense of partnership between the labour and capital. Although, the interest of the employers and employees may clash, still there is a scope for co-operation. According to Hill, whatever may be laid down under labour laws, it is the approach of employers and trade union leaders which matters, and both are enlightened, industrial harmony is not possible.

Collective bargaining is said to be an outstanding feature of economic democracy. It is a two way two party procedure for arriving at a commonly agreed solution. Basically collective bargaining is a method by which management and labour may explore each other's problems, understand view points and develop a framework of employment relations within which both may carry on their day to day activities in a spirit of co-operation, goodwill for their mutual benefit.

According to Dale Yoder, "Collective bargaining is essentially a process in which employees act as a group in seeking to shape conditions and relationships in their employment".

The Encyclopedia of Social sciences defines "Collective bargaining as a process of discussion and negotiations between two parties one or both of whom is a group of persons acting in concert. The resulting bargain is an understanding as to terms and conditions under which a continuing service is to be performed. More essentially, collective bargaining is a procedure by which an employer or employers and a group of employees agree upon the conditions of work".

R.F. Hoxie states that, "Collective bargaining is a mode of fixing the terms of employment by means of bargaining between an organized body of employees and an employer or an association of employees usually acting through organized agents. The essence of collective bargaining is a bargain between interested parties and not a decree from outside parties.

According to the ILO "Collective bargaining refers to negotiations about working conditions and terms of employment between an employer and a group of employees of one or more employee's organizations with a view to reaching an agreement wherein the terms serve as a code of defining the rights and obligations of each party in their employment relations with one another, fix a large number of detailed conditions of employment, during its validity one of the matters it deals with can, in normal circumstances be given as a ground for a dispute concerning an industrial work.

Thus, collective bargaining leads to an agreement known as "Labour Contract, Union Contract" or "Collective Agreement".

Salient Features of Characteristics of Collective Bargaining

Salient features as explained by **Edward T. Cheyfitz** and others are:

1. Collective bargaining is a collective process or group action in which representatives of employer or managers and of employees participate mutually.
2. It is flexible and dynamic process, as it is in the nature of 'give and take' process, party takes a rigid stand.

3. It is a continuous process which is necessary to maintain stable and healthy relationship between the management and the workers. So, it is said that the conclusion of one agreement is in fact beginning of the next collective bargaining.
4. Collective bargaining is a bi-partite process because in its process, two parties are involved. The worker's representatives and the representatives of the management sit together and discuss the issues involved directly through face to face negotiations.
5. As a process, it includes preparing list of issues relating to both the parties, presenting the issues for which viewpoints are generally conflicting, collection of necessary data, understanding each other's view points, arriving at a mutually acceptable decision etc.
6. It is described as an ideal method for promoting industrial jurisprudence. It means management should be conducted by rules rather than by authority decisions. It is a method of enforcing citizenship rights in industry and involves collective control in management.
7. It is also a good interdisciplinary system of handling disputes during the tendency of agreement and of determining, after its expiry, whether a dispute should be re-opened or whether a strike or lockout should be resorted to or not.
8. According to Dunlop, it is a method of settling disputes during the tendency agreement and of determining, after its expiry, whether a dispute should be re-opened or whether a strike or lockout should be resorted to or not.
9. Collective bargaining, as a technique, is useful for satisfying the needs and goals of the workers and management. Hence, it is considered as integral part of industrial society.

10. It is a special type of transaction. The simple 'take it or leave it' type of transaction takes place the form of negotiation between labour and the management.
11. So McConnell and other state that collective bargaining involves symiotics relationship between the two parties, *i.e.* a relationship which simultaneously involves elements of both co-operation and competition.
12. Collective bargaining is not a competitive process but it is a complementary process because each party need something which other party has and hence both the parties come together without which common objectives cannot be achieved.
13. It is an art or an advanced form of human relations where both the parties with conflicting goals come together for mutual benefit and understand each others positions and arrive at a decision which is beneficial not only to both the parties but also to the society at large. It helps to promote industrial peace which is most essential to promote industrial development at an accepted rate in a developing country like India.

Scope of Collective Bargaining

Although the scope of collective bargaining varies from organization to organization, certain issues are observed to be common in negotiations for collective bargaining. According to Taylor, "The essence of free collective bargaining is that the scope of the relationship, the procedures for negotiations and joint dealings and the substantive terms of employment are all private matters to be worked out by the unions and the management without government interference or direction".

The scope of collective bargaining has been steadily increasing on account of several reasons. Randle has stated following reasons for it.

1. The growing strength of unions, which have pressurized managements to include new subjects in the agreements.
2. Increased profits have led to favourable response to the demands of the employees.
3. Increased price along with increased production have contributed to expansion in the subjects for collective bargaining.
4. The liberal and sympathetic attitude evident in the decisions of the courts and legislative enactments have also favoured this expansion.

This list may add that the increase in literacy levels of the workers and awareness about their rights, worker's representatives have to be aware about protecting their rights especially in the gains of higher productivity, whereas management insists upon duties and responsibilities of the workers. Hence this becomes as important issue in the process of collective bargaining.

In early days, the process of collective bargaining was simple. It was concluded in the form of a written document, signed by the representatives of both labour and management, so to be binding on both the parties. It is a legal contract dealing with the rights and obligations of bothe the parties. The agreement covers issues related to: (*i*) Employment and working conditions; (*ii*) Labour welfare, recruitment and management matters; and (*iii*) Organizational matters.

The first two cover wages, bonus, D.A., retirement benefits, working hours, holidays with leave, supply of subsidized essentials like food, transport, housing etc; which are 'Workers interest-oriented' in nature.

The third item deals with union recognition, exclusive bargaining rights, check off schemes, worker's participation in management etc. are union interest-oriented matters.

The fact is that the subject matter covered by collective bargaining varies with the maturity of bargaining relationship between the two parties. With maturity of the bargaining relationship, mutual trust and confidence amongst the parties tends to grow and the agreement acts as a means for peaceful settlement of the day to day disputes. When new contracts are negotiated, new subjects of interest may be included in the process of collective bargaining.

As Butler has pointed out, the contract provisions relate to: (*i*) union security; (*ii*) worker security; (*iii*) economic factors; (*iv*) Management protection.

The Indian Institute of Personnel Management (IIPM), Calcutta has suggested that the following facts should be included in the collective agreement.

(*i*) The purpose of the agreement, its scope and definition of important terms.

(*ii*) The rights and responsibilities of management and of the trade union.

(*iii*) Wages, bonus, production norms, leaves, retiring benefits and terms and conditions of service.

(*iv*) Grievance redress procedure.

(*v*) Methods of machinery for the settlement of possible future disputes and,

(*vi*) A termination clause.

Thus, collective bargaining covers: (*i*) Negotiation; (*ii*) Administration; (*iii*) Interpretation; and (*iv*) Application of written agreements between the parties. It also indicates the policies and procedures, which shall govern the determination of fixation of wages, rates of pay, hours of work and other conditions of employment.

On the basis of recent trends in collective bargaining, Randle concludes that "the subject matter of collective bargaining has broadened until it has virtually eliminated the field of the management prerogatives. The area pattern of collective bargaining has moved from simple style plan bargaining to regionwise and finally to dynamic nature of scope of collective bargaining. At the same time, they show how important negotiation has become as an institution. And they further hold promise of an even greater role of collective bargaining.

Importance of Collective Bargaining

The experience of Western countries indicates that mature labour relations characterized by a greater degree of order and stability and sound wage structure has been associated with collective bargaining. In other words, mature collective bargaining contributes significantly towards maintaining industrial peace and order, which is essential for attaining higher rate of growth in developing countries.

Collective bargaining plays a key role in preventing industrial disputes as follows:

1. It helps to increase economic and moral strength of both, the unions and management.
2. It is useful for prompt, fair and better redressal of grievances.
3. It helps in establishing and developing satisfactory conditions of employment.
4. It helps in arriving at the fair rates of wages and norms of working conditions.
5. It helps in maintaining steady flow of production without any interruption on account of strikes, lock-outs etc.
6. It not only enables to achieve higher rate of growth of production and productivity, but also contributes towards maintaining stability and promoting prosperity of industry.
7. It not only helps the organization to find out solution to the problem of sickness but also ensures benefits to both parties through higher profit to organization and more benefits to employee.

8. It provides a flexible approach for adjustment of wages and employment conditions so as to meet the challenges of technological progress and economic changes that are taking place continuously in modern times.
9. Collective bargaining is the only approach that enables the organization to accept and implement democratic principles in most satisfactory way.
10. It helps to develop a system of industrial jurisprudence by introducing civil rights in the field of industry. It ensures that management is carried out according to rules and regulations rather than in an arbitrary fashion.

Advantages of Collective Bargaining

During early days, Trade Unions were considered as necessary evil. But now both the parties or labour and management have realized the key role that unions can play in maintaining industrial peace and promoting productivity.

(i) *Anti-cyclical measure:* Now, it is held that collective bargaining is a good anti-cyclical measure. It is also argued that the great depression of 1930's was caused partly by the inability of the workers to organize and bargain collectively to maintain their wage levels.

(ii) *Extension of democracy to the workplace:* Slichter has argued that collective bargaining establishes a system of industrial jurisprudence or a process of introducing civil rights into industry. It requires that management will be concluded by rules rather than arbitrary decisions. Rules made jointly by both labour and management are much better than superior to those made and imposed by the government, because they are more flexible or elastic in nature and can be easily modified to suit the changes in the circumstances. The people who are really facing the problems are in a better position to make rules than those who are not aware about the problems but make the rules.

(iii) *Promotion of participatory democracy:* The idea of participatory democracy has been widely accepted by the employers as a force for social stability. By way of participating in the formulation of working rules and joining political organizations, workers gain a stake in the system. So any employers support to extend free labour movements in developing countries. They believe that collective bargaining will buffer the spread of revolutionary unionism in developing countries. It is contended that revolutionaries do not make much progress in countries with advance collective bargaining systems.

(iv) *An equalizing system:* Collective bargaining is regarded as an equitable system, because it equalizes power between the workers and the management. Government helps employers to gain power by permitting them to form corporate type of business activities. Hence, it is only equitable to protect workers by allowing them to enjoy their rights to organize and bargain collectively to protect interests of the workers.

Limitation of Collective Bargaining

1. Collective bargaining may generate more problems than solving them. Firstly, there is a problem of strikes. The strike creates a dilemma for those who have accepted the institution of collective bargaining because it is difficult to have collective bargaining without right to strike. At the same time, strikes can inflict considerable damage to public. Although much attention has been paid to the problem of making collective bargaining successful in order to prevent damage caused by strikes, no solution has been found as yet.
2. Since collective bargaining has been based on power and conflict, it does the most for the people who need the least. The skilled workers can protect their incomes while weaker workers, unskilled workers have very

limited ability to form unions and gain the benefits of collective bargaining.

3. Collective bargaining does not contain sufficient provision for safeguarding the public interest, which might be ignored by collusion between strong unions and employers to fix prices. In USA, where "Collective bargaining is a feature of industrial relations, it is claimed that is has impeded the economy's growth; imparted an upward drift to the general price level and periodically imperiled the nation's health and safety".

However, collective bargaining is widely accepted because of the following reasons:

(*i*) Collective bargaining provides a means to create normative system for regulating industrial conflict and ensuring that it is kept within acceptable limits.

(*ii*) Collective bargaining enables parties to a dispute to view the situation dispassionately. It allows to pause for thought and review the consequences of possible causes of action.

(*iii*) Collective bargaining absorbs energy for betterment, which otherwise would have misdirected. So, Harbisan states that collective bargaining provides a drainage channel for worker's dissatisfaction.

(*iv*) Collective bargaining, by providing a forum for meetings between management and unions can help to facilitate better selection and gradual change of social structure to replace tendency towards revolutionary explosions and civil war.

Principles of Collective Bargaining

For the purpose of efficient functioning of collective bargaining, certain principles have been recommended by various authors, which may be summarized as below:

(a) For Unions and the Management

(*i*) Trade union leaders should be given an opportunity for representing their demands, needs, grievances and attitudes of workers before the management, while management should make an attempt to explain the problems faced by it.

(*ii*) Both the parties should realize that the collective bargaining is an ideal method for taking more expedient and intelligent decisions.

(*iii*) Both the parties must possess the competence for bargaining with mutual respect and implanting the agreement or contract ultimately arrived at.

(*iv*) Both the parties should have a genuine spirit of mutual trust, goodwill and desire to arrive at agreeable solution in the interest of all.

(*v*) The leadership involved should be honest, competent and responsible so as to conclude the agreement satisfactorily.

(*vi*) Both should observe and abide by the national and state laws applicable to collective bargaining.

(*vii*) Both the parties should realize that there has to be close correspondence between wages and the general price level in the economy.

(b) For Management

(*i*) Management should adopt an appropriate labour policy and take necessary precautions to see that it is properly followed by all the employees.

(*ii*) Trade unions should be accorded with recognition as bargaining units.

(*iii*) Management should adopt a dynamic approach by way of changing the policies and views according to the changes in the circumstances and should maintain the dignity of the workers.

(*iv*) While dealing with trade union, the management must be just and reasonable.

(*v*) Management should develop the machinery for settlement of the grievances of the workers as quickly as possible, before they develop into a major issues to be handled by them jointly.

(*vi*) If there are more unions in the organization, then the management should prefer the union with majority representation for the purpose of negotiations.

(*vii*) While studying consequences of collective bargaining, the management, instead of concentrating on economic aspects should prefer social aspects of the bargaining.

(c) *For Trade Unions*

1. The unions should not foster anything opposed to democracy at their workplace.
2. The unions should not concentrate only on higher wages, lesser working hours, better working conditions etc. but at the same time should emphasize on increase in production and productivity, elimination of wastes of all types, improving the quality of the product and adopting cost effective measures.
3. Unions should not insists on such demands which are beyond the paying capacity of the organization or which are against the national policies.
4. The unions should strive for raising and maintaining morale of their members at the higher level as possible.
5. Unions should not forget that strike is the weapon of the last resort and they should try to avoid it as far as possible.

Process of Collective Bargaining

Process of collective bargaining involves the following steps or stages:

1. Pre-Negotiation Phase

This is the state before starting the actual bargaining process. At this stage, the management wants to estimate the power and capacity of the labour union. An attempt is also made to collect relevant data and information so that proper base can be prepared for negotiation.

The bi-partite collective bargaining process usually starts with a charter of demands being presented to the management. A fresh charter is submitted upon the expiry of an earlier agreement. If there exists an agreement between management and the union, as is often the case, then till the fresh agreement is signed, the provisions of the existing agreement would continue till it expires.

2. Selection of Negotiators

Both management and the union select their representatives for taking part in the process of negotiations to put forth respective views. For the purpose of effective negotiations, those persons are selected as negotiators who are fully acquainted with the problems on which negotiations are going to be held.

3. Strategy of Bargaining

Before actual negotiations begin, both management and the union representatives go through several intra-organizational bargains. The management has to settle internal policy issues regarding wages, concessions and other changes that they can accept. Secondly, the viability of the firm in terms of profits and labour costs has to satisfy demands of several stakeholders, including shareholders, consumers, suppliers, employees etc. internal strategies have to focus on reconciling these interests and fix priorities for the demands of the several groups from time to time.

Management has to decide basic strategies and policies to be followed at the time of bargaining with union representatives. The representatives of management should get due powers to enter into agreements with workers.

Similarly, union leaders have to decide their strategy and priorities so as to represent a united front at the negotiating table. Gathering necessary data is essential for formulating charter of demands. They may work out quantum of wage increase and other welfare measures while preparing their charter of demands. Problem areas covering multiple employee grievances such as promotion policy, selection norms etc. may be included in the demands of the union. Thus, union leaders also formulate their strategies for participating negotiations effectively.

4. Tactics of Bargaining

The union's charter of demands covering various subjects ranging from wage increase to personnel policies are discussed at the bargaining table. All the demands are taken up item by item where each side presents its case to the best of its ability.

The technique of collective bargaining is based on the principle of "Give and Take". Both the parties aim at gaining more than what they sacrifice. Once all the aspects of contracts are discussed in detail, the decisions acceptable to both are arrived at.

In addition to considering union demands in recent times, management puts forth counter-demands regarding workplace rules. Thus, collective bargaining has become two way process. Hence, maintaining communication links during negotiations even when the positions are divergent helps in collective bargaining. It also helps to identify "hidden agenda" that one's counterpart is trying to communicate or to read between the lines. The good negotiator has a feel of the situation and uses his knowledge and intelligence to understand the situation. He can predict arguments of the opposite side on various issues and hence develops the most effective strategy to make bargaining successful.

5. Contract Stage

During this stage, both the parties after detailed discussion and through the process of give and take, are now ready to enter into a collective agreement. Such agreement is applicable to a certain fixed period of time, and cover all the details of job security, grievance handling procedure, policies relating to transfers, promotions etc. and rules regarding layoff and retrenchment, hours of work, rules for leaves, incentive schemes, security and health managerial liability etc.

6. Implementation Stage

This is the last stage of the process of collective bargaining. The agreements arrived at through bargaining between the management and the labour unions are to be implemented effectively. Both the parties have no honour these agreements and implement them properly.

The Main Clauses in Collective Bargaining/Subject Matter of Collective Bargaining

The clauses covered by the collective bargaining agreement are as follows:

(i) *Recognition or union security clause:* The recognition clause defines the status to be given to the union during the period of agreement.

(ii) *Hours of work clause:* Many agreements include clauses relating to working hours. These clauses may deal with shift arrangements, time off for meals, overtime payment, holidays and related details.

(iii) *Wage clause:* It is the most important and complicated clause in the agreement. It includes the basic wage policy and specific wage agreements. If piece rates are to be paid, then it is necessary to mention the system to be followed in detail. An escalator clause, if included, also appears under this head.

(iv) *Seniority clause:* It explains the system of seniority and the importance of seniority rights in the context of promotions, selection of vacation periods, choice of shifts and other privileges.

(v) *Other clauses:* It includes other clauses relating to grievance procedures, leaves of absence, welfare funds, shop rules, training of apprentices, disciplinary actions etc.

Various Types of Collective Bargaining

Labour management relations were perceived as being marked by a great deal of conflict. However recently their has been emphasis on labour management co-operation. During negotiation parties can take position and where along a broad spectrum of conflict to co-operation according different types of bargaining originate in the process, which may be discussed as follows:

(a) Distributive or Conjunctive or Traditional Bargaining

It is the most common type of bargaining. It may be defined as "the complex system of activities instrumental to the attainment of one party's goals when they are in basic conflict with those of other party". It is the negotiation in which one party's gain is the other party's loss. For example wage issues are of this type, as every additional rupee paid to employees means a loss of one rupees in profit for the management.

(b) Integrative or Co-operative Bargaining

It refers to activities instrumental to the attainment of objectives which are not in fundamental conflict with those of the other party, such objectives define an area of common concern, under integrative bargaining collaborative problem solving is possible where both the parties gain. For example gain sharing programmes or joint labour management programme to improve the quality of work life, providing retraining for employees with obsolete skill etc.

(c) Intraorganisational Bargaining

It is the process of resolving differences or finding areas of common agreement among members of the same party. For example, union negotiation must decide on their priorities and secure the ratification of a tentatively negotiated agreement. Thus they have to sell the settlement to their own members or even all the negotiations. Significant different may arise regarding preferences and priorities of bargaining.

(d) Single Plant Bargaining

It is the bargaining between management and a single trade union. This type of bargaining is common in USA and India.

(e) Multiple Plant Bargaining

It is the bargaining that takes place between a single factory and establishment having several plants where the workers are employed.

(f) Multiple Employer Bargaining

It is a bargaining between all the trade unions of workers in the same industry through their federal organization as well as employer's federation. This is useful at local or regional level. This is common in industries like textile industry.

(g) Productivity Bargaining

The typical approach in collective bargaining process is that labour makes demands and management makes counter offers to those demands. For example, labour demands 12 per cent increase in pay while company is ready to offer 8 per cent increase only.

Productivity bargaining would change managerial stance to one of the volunteering wage increases provided the union would accept new work practices that will increase productivity of labour and efficiency of the company.

Under productivity bargaining mode is distributive type rather than integrative types. Employers may be forced to pay one time premium for the right to introduce efficiency enhancing programmes. The workers as speeding up of workers or hard work took earlier productivity for employees. But today it is regarded as a key to the progress in modern competitive world. It is held as a way to preserve some jobs in face of foreign competition. Now increase in productivity is shared at 40 per cent by management and 20 per cent by the society in the form of quality products at fair prices.

(h) In India Collective Bargaining is Classified into Four Types as follows

(i) *Settlement under the industrial dispute act:* It includes agreements, which are negotiated by officers during the course of conciliation proceedings.

(ii) *Self-settlement:* Agreement concluded by the parties themselves without reference to a board of conciliation and is signed by them copies of such agreements are sent to appropriate government authorities and also to conciliation officers.

(iii) *Consent awards:* It covers the agreement that are negotiated by the parties on a voluntary basis when disputes are sub judice and which are later submitted to industrial tribunals, labour courts or labour arbitrators for incorporation into the documents as part of awards.

(iv) *Voluntary agreements:* These are the agreements, which are finalized after direct and free negotiation between labour and management and are purely voluntary in character. Their enforcement depends upon good will morale force and co-operation the parties concerned.

Collective Bargaining in India

Collective bargaining was adopted in India in 1952 and it soon became popular. Initially the technique of collective bargaining was used for determining the rates of wages and conditions of employment in case of the most of the sector of the economy.

Since last decade the bargaining strategies have changed and now they deal with non-traditional issues like providing better welfare facilities fringe benefits etc. now the emphasis is no matters like home rent allowance, leave travel concessions educational allowance etc.

Factors Promoting Growth of Collective Bargaining in India

Collective bargaining in India developed along with the development of trade union in India. The first such agreement was made at Ahmedabad Cotton Textile Industry with a view to regulate management labour relationships. However it was only after independence that collective bargaining started making some progress. But the process remained only at plant level and organizational level and not at industry level like in Western countries. The main factors responsible for it progress were-

(*i*) Government measures like schemes of workers education, labour participation in management, the code of efficiency and welfare, code of discipline etc.

(*ii*) Voluntary measures such as tripartite conference, industrial committees, joint consultative boards' etc.

(*iii*) Statutory provisions which had stated certain principles of negotiation, procedure for collective agreement etc.

(*iv*) The industrial truce resolution 1962, which emphasized co-operation between labour and management to dissolve their disputes peacefully.

(*v*) The amendment of the Industrial Disputes Act, 1964 which provided for the termination of an award or settlement only when a proper notice to that effect was given by a majority of workers and not by a trade unions representing minority.

Obstacles of Efficient Functioning of Collective Bargaining in India

The factors hindering the functioning of collective bargaining are:

(*i*) The failure of both parties to develop enough time and energy for preparation for collective bargaining.

(*ii*) Lack of factual information.

(*iii*) Using unfair practices.

(*iv*) Unwillingness of either party to assume the responsibility that are inherent in the process of bargaining.

(*v*) The unequal strength of parties. For collective bargaining both parties need to be equally strong.

(*vi*) Failure of some employees to accept trade unions as a permanent feature of the national economy.

(*vii*) Separatist tendencies of the trade unions.

(*viii*) Failure of government to make strong efforts for development of collective bargaining.

(*ix*) Now adjudication is easily accessible so that collective bargaining is losing its importance.

(*x*) Political interference making unions weaker due to inter union rivalries.

(*xi*) Negative attitude of management towards unions, they prevent workers joining unions. Hence unions remain weak bodies.

Causes of Slow Progress of Collective Bargaining in India

Collective bargaining in India developed as a result of statutory provisions, voluntary measures, Industrial Truce

Resolution 1962 and the amendments of the Industrial Disputes Act 1947. Still it has been observed that the progress is not satisfactory, because of the following reasons.

(a) Union-Related Problems

It is the strength of the participating trade union that determines the effectiveness of the bargaining process. Indian Trade Union even today are relatively weak on account of several limitation. A weak union cannot present its issues forcefully during negotiations.

Many a times workers and trade union leaders are not able to take a unanimous stand while negotiating.

(b) Management Related Problem

In India, management generally has negative attitude towards workers. They do not like attempts of workers. They do not like attempts of workers to form an association which management takes as a threat to their authority, without wholehearted support of the management. Workers find it difficult to form a strong and stable union and because of absence of strong trade union collective bargaining process is adversely affected.

(c) Government Related—Problem

Indian government has failed to create an environment and motivate workers to form a strong trade union and participate actively in the process of collective bargaining. Instead the government has imposed several restrictions on strikes and lockouts, which has in effect discouraged the development of collective bargaining process in India. Similarly adjudication has been made easily accessible, hence parties prefer it rather than going for collective agreement. In other words, collective bargaining has lost its importance.

(d) Political Dominance

Indian trade union is characterized by its political activities rather than making efforts to protect interests of worker. Most of the unions are affiliated to political parties hence the parties use the union to protect their selfish interests rather than workers economic interests.

Various Measures for the Healthy (Future) Prospects of Collective Bargaining in India

Recommendations of the National Commission of Labour to make collective bargaining more effective.

The NCL in 1969 made the recommendations as follows:

(*i*) Government intervention in industrial relations especially in the settlement of industrial disputes should be reduced gradually to the minimum possible extent. Compulsory adjudication of disputes should be used only as a last resort.

(*ii*) Trade union should be strengthened both organizationally and financially by amending the trade union membership fee, reduce the presence of outsiders in the union executive and among the office bearers and increase the minimum number of members in respect of union applying for registration.

(*iii*) A separate legislation be enacted for existing legislation be amended for:

(*a*) Compulsory recognition of trade unions and certification of unions as bargaining agents.

(*b*) Prohibition and penalization of unfair labour practices.

(*c*) Bargaining in good faith by both employers and union.

(*d*) Making collective agreement legally valid.

In addition P. Subba Rao has given suggestions as follows for making functioning of collecting bargaining still more effective.

(1) There must be change in the attitude of employers and employees. They should settle their differences on their own taking help of outsiders or going for litigation.

(2) Collective buying is best conducted at plant level. The representatives of both the parties should be determined to arrive at an agreed solution of their respective problem.

(3) Both the parties should enter upon negotiations on demands for reaching an agreement.

The union should not put towards unreasonable demands. Any refusal to negotiate should be held as unfair practice. Rigid attitudes are not suitable for collective bargaining.

(4) Negotiations can be successful only when the parties rely or facts and figures to support their agreements. The trade union may be assisted by specialists like economists, productivity experts, professional etc. to present their view to management properly.

(5) Both the parties should avoid unfair labour practices. The negotiations should be conducted under the atmosphere of good will.

(6) When negotiations results agreements the term of contract should be put down in writing and embodies in a document. If no agreement is reached, then the parties should agree to conciliation mediation or arbitration. If it also fails then the workers are allowed this right will defeat the process of collective bargaining.

(7) Once agreement is reached, it must be honoured and fairly implemented. No strike or lockout should be permitted in respect of issues, which have already been covered in the contract, and the union should not be allowed to raise fresh demands.

(8) A provision for arbitration should be incorporated in the agreement, which should be come operative when

there is any disagreement on the interpretation of its terms and conditions. Third party decision should be a final and binding one.

Indian Institute of Personnel Management Offered the following Suggestions

(*i*) A truly representative, enlightened and strong trade union should come into being and should function on strictly constitutional lines.

(*ii*) There should be a progressive and strong management, which is conscious of its obligations and responsibilities to the owners of the business, to the employees, the consumers and the country.

(*iii*) There should be unanimity between labour and management on the basic objectives of the organization and of the workers and a mutual recognition of their rights and obligations.

(*iv*) When there are several units of the company, there should be a delegation of authority to the local management.

(*v*) A fact finding approach and a willingness to use new tools such as industrial engineering should be adopted for the solution of industrial problem.

Thus it may be concluded that there is beginning of voluntary collective bargaining in India at plant level. The negotiations at state or at industry level are not frequent. There is a need to develop voluntary collective agreement for mutual interest of both the parties.

Levels of Collective Bargaining Agreements

In India collective bargaining agreements take place at three levels.

(*i*) At plant level.

(*ii*) At industry level.

(*iii*) At national level.

A. At Plant Level

The plant level agreement is applicable to that plant only. It covers certain norms of conduct for maintaining good labour management relations and eliminating misunderstanding. It aims at providing easy and quick solutions for urgent issues.

Examples.

In India are:

(*i*) The Bata Shoe Co. Agreement (1955).

(*ii*) The Tata Iron and Steel Company (1956).

(*iii*) Modi Spinning and Weaving Mills Co. Agreement (1956)

(*iv*) Celtics India (1959) etc.

B. At the Industry Level

The industry level agreement was settled in case of the textile industry in Bombay and Ahmedabad.

The agreement between the Ahmedabad Mill-owners Association and the Ahmedabad Textile Labour Association (1955) laid down the procedure to be followed for the grant bonus and the voluntary settlement of industrial disputes.

This agreement was applicable to all the member mills of the association and it covered the period for four years 1953-57. It was decided that the Bonus will be paid out of the surplus or profit at a rate of not less than 4.8 per cent and not more than 25 per cent, of the basic wage earned during a given year. It was also agreed of bonus to be distributed by each mill. In case of any dispute the matter was to be referred to the President of the Labour Appellate Tribunal or a person acceptable to both parties.

Under the Second Agreement it was agreed by both the association that all industrial disputes in future between the members of two association were to be settled through mutual negotiation. If it failed the arbitration will be adopted. But no party will go for settlement through courts.

C. At the National Level

The National Level agreement is bipartite in nature and finalized at conference of labour and management convened by the Government of India. The example of such agreements are:

(*i*) The Delhi Agreement Feb. 1951.

(*ii*) Bonus Agreement for Plantation Workers Jan. 1956.

The Delhi Agreement was settled during the conference of the representative of both, labour and management, it dealt with rationalization and the related matters.

The Bonus Agreement for plantation workers was concluded in Jan. 1956 between representatives of the Indian Tea Association and India Planters Association and Hind Mazdoor Sabha and INTUC. The agreement dealt with the problem of payment of bonus to about one million plantation workers.

CHAPTER 5

Participation in Management

Workers Participation in Management

The Second Five Year Plan started several progressive trends in the field of labour policy where one important concept was that of workers participation in management of increased association of labour with management. The second plan aimed at the establishment of socialist society. The plan stated that the creation of industrial democracy is a prerequisite for the establishment of a socialist society. The idea of associations labour with management is not new. In India progressive industrial establishments had already accepted it. Even the Industrial Disputes Act, 1947 provides for setting up of works committees. Thus since second plan there has been significant progress in the field of association workers with management.

According to Kesari, the concept of workers participation in management is an essential ingredient of industrial democracy and indicates an attempt on the part of and employer to build his employees into a team which work towards realization of common objective. The term industrial democracy has thus generally been accepted in the sense of workers participation in management.

Ian Clegg states that workers participation in management implies a situation where workers representatives are, to some extent, involved in the process of management decision-making, but where the ultimate power is the hands of management.

K.C. Alexander considers, "a management to be participative if it gives scope to workers to influence its decision making process on any level". The concept of industrial democracy may be defined "as a system of communication and consultation, either formal or informal by which the employees of the organization are kept informed of the affairs of the undertaking and through which they express their opinions and contribute of managerial decisions".

According to Davis, worker's participation in management is a metal and emotional involvement of person in a group situation which encourages him to contribute to goals and share responsibilities in them".

The workers' participation in management is basically a mechanism through which workers have a say in the decision making process of an enterprise.

Preston and Post described three stages or revolutions of management development. Hence, first managerial revolution took place when management started appearing itself as a specialized function within hierarchical organizations.

The second revolution was characterized by professionalisation of management, which was encouraged by the growth of industrial organization and the complexity and dynamism of managerial tasks.

The third revolution is the contemporary revolution characterized by workers' participation in management.

According to Ghosh participation is not merely to protect and further one's interests but is a system of checks and balances on both the groups which requires a great sense of responsibilities and educated awareness to cope with the several aspects of the participative system.

The international institute of labour studies define it as "The participation results from practices which increase the scope of the employee's share of influence in decision-making at different tiers of the organizational hierarchy with concomitant assumption of responsibility.

Objectives of Workers' Participation in Management

The main objectives may be stated as follows:

(*i*) It is a measure of improving efficiency of the company and establishing harmonious industrial relations.

(*ii*) It aims at improving productivity of the workers not only for the advantage but also for the society as a whole.

(*iii*) To promote better understanding among employees about their role and place and the process of attainment of organizational goals.

(*iv*) To satisfy workers social and esteem needs.

(*v*) To promote co-operation between labour and management in order to maintain industrial peace and harmony.

(*vi*) From ideological point of view it aims at development of self management in industry.

(*vii*) To build most dynamic and creative human resource.

(*viii*) To build the economic nation though entrepreneurship and development.

(*ix*) In ethical context participation is designed to promote individual development accordance with the concept of human rights dignity. Thus it has ethical economic social political psychological objectives which should be fulfilled.

Characteristics/Features of Worker's Participation in Management

Main Characteristics

(*i*) The concept of workers participation in management involves workers management and government hence is viewed differently by different agencies.

(*ii*) The movement of participation is rapidly spreading throughout the world hence it called as global movement.

(*iii*) The participation movement is the result of economic, political, social, cultural industrial, psychological, etc. forces which made it popular in all the countries of the world.

(*iv*) According to some thinkers it's a tool for maintaining healthy relations between labour management. So it provides a foundation for developing industrial democracy.

(*v*) Other thinkers consider it as a movement for removing present system of management and ownership of business organizations.

(*vi*) The idea of participation emerged as an alternative for exploitative and unjust capitalist system of management on account of:

(*a*) The threats from labour unions with countervailing power especially in organized sector.

(*b*) The demands of continuous production during world wars when the managers developed strategies to maintain uninterrupted flow of production in the economy.

(*c*) Demand placed by the successive economic plans on both management and labour to attain accelerated growth of production and productivity in order to promote the process of economic development in the country.

(*d*) Under the impact of trusteeship concept, Gandhiji it was expected that the workers and management should come together and work as a trustee of the resources under their control for maximization of welfare in the economy.

(*e*) It is considered as a right step in the direction of establishment of socialistic pattern of society through industrial democracy.

(*vii*) Several other factors also led to the growth for participation such as:

(*i*) Growth of public sector enterprise.

(*ii*) Development of scientific management, which insisted upon close co-operation between labour and management for increasing productivity.

(*iii*) Experiments in industrial psychology.

(*iv*) Positive role of the ILO, leading to a closer collaboration between employers and employees.

Advantages of Participation (or Case for)

According to Pyle, participation provides greater autonomy for subordinates and leads to increase in motivation for:

(*i*) More balanced interaction pattern leading to lower resistance to innovation and technological change.

(*ii*) It helps members of the group to unfreeze their attitude and engageed productive activities wholeheartedly.

(*iii*) It permits leaders to strengthen them their position. They can enhance their status both by taking a leading part in making the decision and through inducing group member to follow it.

(*iv*) It enables the subordinates to take advantage of an exchange relationship as boss listens to them and allows them to be corrected.

(*v*) It provides an opportunity to subordinates to demonstrate their skills and learns and have experience.

(*vi*) It subjects the individual to the group pressure to implement the decision taken by the group.

(*vii*) It satisfies the urge of the subordinates of self- expression and improve their self-image by association with decision-making.

(*viii*) It bring about qualitative change in the attitudes of the parties so that suspicion is replaced by mutual trust antagonism by understanding and a stable, durable workable relationship is built up that promotes industrials peace.

(*ix*) It may lead to the change in the organizational structure by transferring the management function entirely to the workers so as to develop self management.

(*x*) It is described as a device for promoting social education for developing solidarity among working communities and for tapping latent human resources.

(*xi*) It is claimed to be essential on economic social and psychological grounds.

(*xii*) It helps in extending mutual understanding between two parties usually at conflict.

(*xiii*) It may help workers to adjust themselves to change rather than resisting the change.

(*xiv*) It provides opportunity to workers to demonstrate and develop their talents.

The various Models of Worker's Participation in Management

Models of Workers' Participation

The scheme of workers participation may take any form depending upon extent to which management accepts the involvement of representatives of workers in the process of decision-making. On this basis the following forms emerge which are described as participation models.

1. Information sharing model.
2. Consultation model.
3. Association of workers models.
4. Joint decision-making model.
5. Collective bargaining model.
6. Works councils model.
7. Joint management council model.

8. Workers self management model.
9. Ascending participation model.
10. Descending participation model.

1. ***Information sharing model:*** Under this model the workers have an access only to the information about their organization regarding its various activities, plans, procedures such information may be provided to the employees in a large organization through house journal, pamphlets, in-house training etc. but the workers are not given opportunity to exercise their influence over the process of decision-making of the management under idea sharing scheme the management is ready to accept useful ideas suggested by workers publicity and may reward to motivate others to suggest creative ideas.
2. ***Consultation models:*** Under this approach the management in case of certain matter before taking decisions consults the workers. These matters include changes in existing amenities, work method etc. thus the workers are only consulted but the management, which is bound to accept advice or suggestion given by the workers, take the decisions.
3. ***Association of workers model:*** Under this model the representatives of the workers are able to influence the decision-making process of the management it may take different forms like safety committee, canteen committee, workers committee etc. however the ultimate responsibility to take decision rests with the management.
4. ***Joint decision-making model:*** It is the highest level of participation as it involves both the parties to take decision jointly and administer it jointy. The items on which such decisions are taken are not only those related to workers but are also those of common interest such as cost and wastage's reduction, improvement in

efficiency and productivity, etc. this scheme is more popular amongst employees.

5. ***Association of workers model:*** It provides the workers and management the right through collective agreement to lay down certain rules both for formulation and termination of contract of employment and conditions of service in the organization. It is considered as an important tool in the hands of labour of influencing managerial decision.
6. ***Work council model:*** Work councils are constituted of the representatives of the workers only. There may be one council for the whole firm or a hierarchy of council from shop floor to the staff board.
7. ***Joint management council model:*** This council consists of the representatives of the workers and management and they may functions as advisory bodies to influencing decision-making. In India its role is advisory and consultative.
8. ***Workers self management model:*** It is a popular scheme in Yogoslavia. Where there is a substantial degree of workers' participation in the main decision-making bodies there may be a system of workers ownership or the workers may have right to use the assets of the organization.
9. ***Ascending participation model:*** Where the workers are given an opportunity to participate actively in the decision-making process at higher levels through their representatives elected for work councils. It is also known as integrated participation.
10. ***Descending participation model:*** Under this type of participation the workers are given more power to plan and arrive at decision about their own work. It involves the elements of both delegation and job enrichment.

However the most important forms of participation are:

(*i*) Collective Bargaining

(*ii*) Joint administration

(*iii*) Joint decision-making

(*iv*) Joint consultation

(*v*) Information sharing.

G.L. Nanda after studying various models or forms of workers participation schemes in several countries of the world concluded that:

(*a*) Though there was a variety of forms in which consultation between the management and workers was maintained, the in built character of consultation is the single important factor in their success.

(*b*) There was no attempt to by pass trade unions through the establishment of joint consultation machinery.

Evaluation of the Participation Scheme in India

Although the Government supports the concept of participative management in principle, employers and employees no body is showing serious interest in the serious interest in the scheme. A welfare state makes an attempt to make some progress in this direction but on accounting lack of proper co-operation and support by the concerned parties the scheme has failed to make significant impact on the industrial scene in India.

It has been observed that the workers representatives are more interested in enlargement of their amenities and facilities relating to grievances, higher wages, better conditions of work-security of service than with major problems, like reducing the rate of absenteeism, increasing productivity, efficient utilization of plant and equipment etc; in addition in majority of the cases the joint management council are not functioning effectively.

The main reasons that account for failure of the participation scheme may be listed as follows:

1. Lack of strong trade unionism.
2. Unhappy and strained industrial relations.
3. Illiteracy and ignorance of the workers.
4. Non-cooperative attitude of litigation minded worker's representatives.
5. Excessive delays in the implementation of the decision of participative bodies.
6. Multiplicity of participative forums such as works committee, joint management council, shop council, unit council, canteen committee-safety committee, suggestions committee etc. each will ill-defined role and functions create confusion increasing in duplication of efforts leading to wastage of time and energy. All these contribute towards failure of the scheme.
7. Failure to develop the spirit of participation by the parties as the employers consider bipartite bodies as substitutes for trade unions while employees look at it as their rival. This creates hostility and jealousy among.
8. There is difference in approach to the scheme as the employers feel that the participation scheme should be introduced in stages while employees insist that the scheme should be introduced at all the levels at the same time. Hence the scheme are accepted with reservation.
9. Progressive employees who have already developed a system of communication and consultation with their employees find such bodies to be superstitious and useless.
10. The joint management councils were created without creating a congenial and constructive climate for them.
11. Lack of follow-up measures by the government agency for the implementations of the scheme especially with referrence to the setting up of works committees under the provisions of the industrial democracy. They are

not ready to give recognition to the representative union as official representatives of the workers, even though in Maharashtra necessary legislation is in operation.

12. The attitude of the management towards the scheme is also not favourable because they consider these schemes as concessions given to the workers and not as a measure of establishing industrial democracy. They are not ready to give recognition to the representative union as official representatives of the workers, even though in Maharashtra necessary legislation is in operation.
13. As Monoappa has pointed out the attitude of the union towards the scheme and the lack of understanding on the part of the union is a limitation. Trade unions hold the view that as the workers are lacking is higher level of education, political consciousness, social unity co-operative participation might destroy the unity of labour movement itself. It is necessary to develop right type of attitudes on the part of both the parties through education and training of workers and managers at one level.

Walker has concluded that, "worker's participation in management schemes would be successful only when there is a transition from structural participation to living participation or active participation by the parties and interaction between worker's representatives and managers".

Suggestions to Make the Participation Scheme Effective in India

The following are the suggestions for making the participation scheme successful in India.

(*i*) The management should adopt progressive attitude and recognize its responsibilities and obligations towards workers and trade unions.

(*ii*) There should a strong active democratic representative sound union to represent the cause of workers along with protecting the interest of the organization.

(*iii*) Both the parties should behave in such a way that it will promote the climate of mutual trust and faith among all the parties concerned.

(*iv*) All the parties concerned in participative management should be well prepared to participate at all the levels.

(*v*) The participative scheme should be mutually formulated with precise objectives in view.

(*vi*) There should be two way effective communications between both the parties and free and constructive consultation of workers by the management.

(*vii*) Both the parties should accept the party's scheme as a challenge and try their level best to make it effective through proper implementation.

(*viii*) It is the responsibility of management and the government to provide necessary facilities for training the task of participative management efficiently and effectively.

(*ix*) Both the parties should anticipate the benefits of the scheme and be prepared to implement the schemes successfully.

(*x*) The schemes of participation should emerge out of need felt by the parties involved so that there will be higher level to commitment on the part of all the parties.

(*xi*) The participation programme should not be considered as necessary additions but it has to be integrated into the process of collective bargaining so that it may lead to stable and workable relations is the organization.

Industrial Democracy

Industrial Democracy: To maintain sound industrial relations, industrial democracy must be maintained. The following principles should be followed for maintaining industrial democracy.

(*i*) Recognition of the dignity of the individual and his right to personal freedom and equality of opportunity.

(*ii*) Mutual respect, confidence, understanding, goodwill and acceptance of responsibility on the part of both employer, management and workers and their representatives in the exercise of the rights and duties in operation of the industry.

(*iii*) Similarly, there has to be an understanding between the various orgnizations of employers and employees who represent the management and workers.

Industrial Peace

Industrial Peace: Permanent industrial peace in an organization is most essential which can be ensured through the following measures:

(*i*) Machinery for the prevention and the settlement of industrial disputes: It included legislative and non-legislative measures. Preventive measures include works committees, standing orders, welfare officers, shop councils, joint councils and joint management councils. Settlement methods include voluntary arbitration, conciliation and adjudication.

(*ii*) Powers to the government: Government should be provided with the authority of settling the industrial disputes when they are settled between the two parties and also by voluntary arbitration.

(*iii*) Provision for the bipartite and tripartite committees: In order to evolve personnel policies, code of conduct, code of discipline etc.

(*iv*) Provision for the various committees: In order to implement and evaluate the collective bargaining agreements court orders and judgments, awards of the voluntary arbitration etc. there should be provision for the committees.

CHAPTER 6

Grievance Handling Procedure

Bi-Partite Bodies

The origin of the Bi-partite bodies may be traced back to 1920 when a few joint committees were set up in Government presses. In Tata Iron and Steel Company (TISCO) such committees were setup. In 1922 the workers people's welfare committee was established in the textile mills at Madras for achieving and maintaining close contact with workers. Some private organizations and railways established such committees. During the period of Second World War these committees played an important role.

The Industrial Truce Resolution 1947 also emphasized the establishment of such committees in each industrial undertaking. As a result Industrial Dispute Act, 1947 under Section 3 (i) provides for setting up works committee of the representatives of the workers and management in all the undertaking employing 100 or more workers.

Even the First and Second five years plans stressed the need of the establishment of the bipartite committees in industrial organization with a view to increasing production, improving the quality of the products, reducing cost of production and eliminating wastes.

The two important committees are Work Committee and Joint Management Councils, which have done their job effectively.

Objectives and Functions

Work committees are the bipartite bodies formed by the enterprises employing 100 or more workers for the purpose of prevention and settlement of industrial dispute at the unit level. Works committees are known as the most effective social institutions.

Objectives

(*i*) To remove the causes of friction in day-to-day work situation by providing an effective grievance handling procedure.

(*ii*) To adopt measures for securing amity and good relationships.

(*iii*) To help in the process of establishing continuing bargaining relationship.

(*iv*) To strengthen the spirit of voluntary settlement.

These committees were successful in developing a greater sense of participation and promote the spirit of co-operation between workers and management. They can provide a channel for mutual interaction that helps in keeping tension very low and create suitable atmosphere for negotiation.

The works committees also provide facilities for unions to know about the working of the organization and increase awareness about discipline and efficiency. These committees try to manage the operations of the private industrial units in conformity with national interest and also provide an agency to supervise management of nationalized undertakings. Their contribution in the field of promoting industrial goodwill and harmonious relation has been quite significant.

The meeting of the works committee must be held not less than once in three months. During its first meeting the committee may work out its procedure and practice. It may meet during working hours and the worker attending it may be treated as on duty.

The employer has to submit six monthly programme report regarding constitution and working of the works committee in the prescribed form to the concerned conciliation officer.

Functions of Works Committee

According to Section 3 (1) (2) of the Industrial Dispute Act, the works committees, "promote measures for securing and preserving an amity and good relations between the employer and the workmen, and to that end, comment upon matters of their common concern or interest and endeavour to compose any material difference of opinion in respect of such matters.

Thus the works committees not only secure co-operation from employees but also help in promoting industrial good will. They provide popular agency to supervise the management of nationalized undertakings.

In India the legal requirements and government encouragement led to setting up of a large number of works committees in several undertakings. However it is observed that in spite of legal support they are not effective. Many employees believe that the works committees are substitutes for trade union while the trade unions treat them as rivals. This has resulted into failure of works committees to function effectively. Many works committees exist on paper and they neither meet not do any useful work. It has been pointed out that the committees were assigned a large number of functions which created uncertainty and confusion among workers and management. Similarly the composition of the committee is also a very elaborate procedure because it involves the election of workers representatives without provision for any recognized union under the act. The general atmosphere in industrial units was that of strained relations and that of atmosphere of distrust, which prevailed, made functioning of such organization very difficult so Giri concludes that the hopes entertained in the works committees as a means of reducing industrial strife and misunderstanding and resolving differences have not been fulfilled.

Role of Joint Management Councils in Promoting Joint Consultation in Industry in India

The origin of the joint management council may be traced back in industrial policy resolution of 1956 where it was emphasized that, "In a socialist democracy, labour is a partner in the common task of development and should participate in it with enthusiasm. There should be joint consultation, workers and technician should whatever possible be associated progressively in management. Enterprises in the public sector have to set an example in this respect".

Functions of Joint Management Councils

Indian Labour Conference in 1957 stated the functions of the council as follows:

(*i*) The council will make an attempt to improve the working and living conditions of the workers;

(*ii*) To improve productivity;

(*iii*) To encourage suggestions from the employees;

(*iv*) To assist in the administration of laws and agreements;

(*v*) To create in the employees a live sense of participation.

The management on the following matters will consult the council.

(*i*) General administration of standing orders and their amendments when needed;

(*ii*) Introduction of new methods of production and manufacturing involving redeployment of men and machinery;

(*iii*) Closure, reduction in or cessation of operations.

The council will have the right to receive information, discuss and give suggestion on

(*i*) General economic situation of the unit.

(*ii*) The state of market, production and sells programmes.

(*iii*) Methods of manufacture and work.

(*iv*) The annual balance sheet and profit and loss statement and connected documents and explanations.

The council will be entrusted with responsibility in respect of:

(*i*) Administration of welfare measures.

(*ii*) Supervision of safety measures.

(*iii*) Operation of vocational training and apprenticeship schemes.

(*iv*) Preparation of schedules of working hours and breaks and holidays.

(*v*) Payment of rewards for valuable suggestion received from employees etc.

Evaluation of Functioning of JMCs

The progress regarding the establishment of JMC in various units in private sector was very poor and even in public sector units. There was no inclination to introduce the scheme of the establishment of the JMC the Government set up a joint consultative machinery at the apex regional and local levels in railways post and tergraphs and defence. Several private sector units especially textile mills, skill mills and cement companies established JMCs.

However, it was observed that the schemes of JMCs were not at all suitable to Indian environment. According to Kennedy, a belief in the workers participation in management is in conflicts with the goals of independent unionism and free collective bargaining. The main reasons of unsatisfactory progress of the JMCs in Indian are:

(*i*) Lack of interest on the part of workers.

(*ii*) Unfavourable attitude of management.

(*iii*) Lack of proper information sharing between workers and management.

(*iv*) Absence of agreement regarding matters on which the JMCs should be consulted.

(*v*) Rivalry between unions.

(*vi*) Inadequate training facilities both for workers and management.

It is interested to note that even the National Commission on labour was not enthusiastic about the scheme. The commission held to view that when the system of union recognition becomes an accepted practice both management and unions will themselves gravitate towards greater co-operation in areas they consider to be of mutual advantage. And set up JMC. However it may be argued that JMCs can play an very useful role in promoting industrial democracy hence it needs to be made more effectively by way of providing necessary conditions for their rapid growth.

Standing Orders

Standing orders are the rules and regulations relative to the condition of employment. In order to develop and maintain healthy industrial relation, clear statement of standing order is desirable.

Standing orders define precisely the conditions of employment and hold the employees liable to make these conditions known by the employees. These orders regulate the conditions of employment, discharge grievances, misconduct, disciplinary action etc. of the workers employed by the organization. There are important issues from the point of view of maintaining healthy relations. Unredressed grievances may develop into industrial disputes and unrest among the employees.

The first legislative enactment in India, which incidentally sought to regulate the standing orders, was the Bombay Industrial Disputes Act, 1938. The government of India enacted the Industrial Employment (standing orders) Act, 1946.

The object of the Act is "to require employers in industrial establishment to define with sufficient precision the condition of employment under them and to make the said conditions known to workmen employed by them". It has been enacted for regulating the conditions of recruitment, discharge disciplinary action holidays of the workers.

A worker is defined as any person (including an apprentice) employed in any industrial establishment to do any skilled or unskilled, manual, supervisory, technical, clerical work for hire or reward but does not include any such person who is mainly employed in a managerial or administrative capacity or a supervisor drawing more than Rs. 500 per month or one whose functions are mainly of the managerial nature. [Section 2 (i)].

Matters to be covered by the standing orders: The schedule I of the act includes the following matters:

(*i*) Classification of employees whether permanent, temporary, apprentices, probationers or badlis.

(*ii*) Manner of notification to employees of the period and hours of work, holidays pay days and wage rates.

(*iii*) Shift working.

(*iv*) Attendance and late coming.

(*v*) Leave and holiday and condition procedure and authority for the grant of these.

(*vi*) Liability to search ad entry into premises through certain gates.

(*vii*) Temporary stoppage of work and rights and liabilities of employers and employees arising there from.

(*viii*) Termination of employment and notice to be given by employer and employee.

(*ix*) Suspension and dismissal for misconduct and acts of omissions which constitute misconduct.

(*x*) Means of redress for employees against unfair treatment or wrong exactions on the part of the employer or his agent or servant.

A. Obligations of the Employer

Regarding standing order the obligation of employer are:

(*i*) To submit draft standing orders with the required information to the certifying officer for certification within the time limit set in the act;

(*ii*) To act in conformity with the certifying standing orders in the day-to-day dealings with the workers;

(*iii*) To modify certified standing orders only with the approval of the certifying offices;

(*iv*) To post prominently the text of the certified standing orders in English or any other language understood by the majority of workmen, near the entrance, through which the majority workers enter the establishment and also in all departments where workmen are employed.

B. Obligations of the Workmen

(*i*) To work in conformity with certified standing orders; and

(*ii*) To comply with the provision of act or Model Standing orders is so far as a modification and interpretation of these orders are concerned.

Thus the standing orders lay down rules about doing rests with the management. Hence the compliance of these standing orders by the workers and union leaders in co-operation with management is essential of maintaining industrial peace and avoiding conflicts in the organizations. Poor administration and faulty application of the standing order may give rise to grievances and misconduct which may disturb industrial relations.

Grievance Handling Procedures Adopted by Indian Organizations

Grievance implies dissatisfaction or distress or suffering or grief caused unnecessarily or illegally. In the context of labour management relations grievance is a complaint or representation made in writing as regard to a company related matters arising from employment or service condition or from condition involving unfair treatment by the employees or from violation of any agreement or standing instructions.

Grievance is defined as a real an imaginary feeling of personal injustice, which an employee has concerning his employment relation.

Redressal of grievances on urgent basis, very promptly is a necessary condition for creating good labour management relations and employing efficiency at the plant level. Grievances should not be allowed to accumulate otherwise they breed further grievances. When grievances go on accumulating with no hopes of immediate solutions may lead to frustration, disloyalty non-co-operation among workers that may affect quantity and quality of the output. This may take the form of higher absenteeism go slow work to rule, demonstration gherao, violence and strikes. Hence proper disposal of grievance needs a serious consideration for harmonious industrial relations and maintenance of industrial peace.

Settlement of Grievances

It has been recognized that these should be the appropriate procedures through which the grievances of workers may be submitted and settled. This recognitions based on consideration of fairness and justice, which require that worker's claims regarding their rights should receive fair and impartial determination and on the desire to remove from the area of power conflict type of dispute that can be settled through authoritative determination of the respective rights and obligations of the parties.

The procedure for settlement of grievances is sometimes established on account of legal. Compulsion order to general agreements between the central organization of employees and employers. In order to make procedure to function effectively it is necessary that the workers should be familiar with it and they should have confidence in the fairness of the management in handling grievances and the procedure should be faster.

Procedure in India

Before the enactment of the Industrial Employment (standing orders) Act, 1946, the settlement of day-to-day grievances of workers in India did not receive much attention.

Under the factories act, 1948 state government had framed rules requiring labour welfare officers to ensure settlement of grievances, but this provision was not effective because of dual role of these officers.

In the past a detailed grievance procedure were worked out only by mutual agreement in few units and most of these units did not have any machinery for the redressal of grievances often resulted into industrial disputes.

In a large undertakings a common type of grievance procedure involves successive steps at different levels, a worker's grievance being first discussed with the immediate supervisor and then if no solution is found, with higher levels of management. The number of steps in procedure varies with the size of the organization. Sometimes an important question of principle involving many workers is concerned; the matter may go up directly to the higher committees within the organization hear grievance after they have been considered at lower levels. A settlement reached jointly by workers and management representatives at any level are generally is regarded as final and binding on both the parties. A grievance is also deemed to be settled if an appeal is not lodged at the next higher level within a given time.

Steps in Handling Grievances

While handling grievances, the following steps are involved:

(*i*) Defining or describing a grievance it inmplies clear statement of the grievance so that it will be fully understood.

(*ii*) Collect all the facts that help to explain how, when, where, why, and to whom the grievance occurred. The executive handling the grievance must know when the alleged grievance was first noticed and whether it has repeated or not and where it took place and the circumstances under which it occurred. This process is necessary to gain the confidence of the employees. The employees should be convinced that the management is quite serious to give justice to the workers involved.

(*iii*) Establish tentative solution to the grievance: after getting the detailed picture of the grievance, next step is to establish a tentative solution and to check whether it works properly or not. If the solution and repeat the process if necessary till the final right solution is find out.

(*iv*) Collect information to check the validity of the tentative solution. It is necessary to verify the tentative solution. The information that is available be collected and attempt has to be made to match it against possible solution.

(*v*) Apply the solution: the executive may hold further conference with aggrived employee and question other employees. Once a final decision is reached it should be immediately applied.

(*vi*) Follow up to make sure that it has been handled effectively and grievance has been disappeared.

Finally the executive has to check whether the employee's attitude has been favourably changed. Once it is so the executive may conclude that the grievance has been settled.

Principles of Handling Grievances

While handling grievances principles need to be followed:

(*i*) Grievance procedure should be fair and just.

(*ii*) The provisions of a grievance procedure should be definite and clear.

(*iii*) The grievance procedure should be simple so that the employees can understand it.

(*iv*) It should function promptly and speedily.

(*v*) Try to show right attitude so that aggrieved employee would have confidence in supervisor.

(*vi*) While handling grievances supervisors must have confidence in themselves and be fully aware of their responsibilities.

(*vii*) Total effects of decision should be considered rather than considering short run effects of the decision.

Essential Features of Model Grievance Procedure

(*i*) An aggrieved worker shall first present his grievance verbally in person to the officer designated by the management for this purpose. An owner shall be given within 48 hours of presentation of complaint.

(*ii*) If the worker is not satisfied with the decision of his officer or fails to receive an answer within the stipulated time period, he shall either in person or accompanied by his departmental representative present his grievance to the head of the department. The head of the department shall give his answer within three days of the presentation of the grievance.

(*iii*) If the decision of the department head is not satisfactory the aggrieved worker may request for the forwarding of his grievance to the grievance committee, which shall make its recommendation to the manager within seven days of the workers request. The management shall implement unanimous recommendation of the grievance committee.

In the even of difference of opinion among the matters of the grievance committee, the views of the members and relevant papers shall be placed before the manager for final decision. In any case the final decision, the final decision of the management shall be communicated to the workmen concerned by the personnel officer within three days from the receipt of the grievance committee's recommendation.

(*iv*) If the decision from the management fails to come within the stipulated period or if the decision is unsatisfactory the worker has a right to appeal to management for revision. A worker may take union officer with him for facilitating discussion with workers revision petition.

(*v*) If any agreement is not still possible then the union and management may refer the grievance with voluntary arbitration within a week of the receipt by the worker of management's decision.

Procedure Adopted for Disciplinary Action in India

Recently, to maintain discipline in the organization has become a serious problem. In most of the industrial units the main constraint is the absence of work culture and work ethos. But the workers cannot develop it alone as the major responsibility and equality of working life it is necessary that union-workers and management should all work together. Discipline is necessary for the well-ordered conduct of any activity. In industry it is most essential because the prosperity of any organization and hence of nation ultimately depends upon the accelerated growth of industrial development. Indiscipline in one sector may lead to indiscipline in other sectors of economy. So spire gal and schedule argue that "discipline is the force that promotes an individual or group to observe rules and regulations and procedures that are deemed necessary to the attainment of an objective".

According to Calhoon, "Discipline may be considered as the force that promotes individuals or groups to observe rules standards and procedures deemed necessary for organization.

Definition

Discipline may be defined as:

(*i*) Means to train to obey implicitly and given order.

(*ii*) A means to train to behave in accordance with rules and regulations.

(*iii*) A technique to bring under controls the people at work.

(*iv*) A means to train to do things in an ordinary way and to establish learning process.

Discipline is necessary to achieve the objectives of:

(*i*) Making members of the organizations accept voluntarily the rules and regulations to achieve the objectives of organizations.

(*ii*) To create the feeling of tolerance and mutual co-operation among persons.

(*iii*) To develop respect for human beings and human relation and to create favourable atmosphere.

Causes of Indiscipline

Employer's non-conformity or refusal to observe the established rules and practices or standard work behaviour is indiscipline. Such deviant behaviour can be observed in the form of such acts as disobedience to supervisor's authority and instructions, apathy to work, unconcern for quality, substandard performance, absenteeism, irregular attendance etc. negative action.

The real causes of indiscipline arise from the experience of the employees from the organization, culture, ideology, and environment. The main factors resulting into indiscipline are:

(*i*) Lack of commitment.

(*ii*) Bad service condition.

(*iii*) Non-fulfilment of economic and social needs.

(*iv*) Social stratification.

(*v*) Alien factory culture.

(*vi*) Poor communication system.

(*vii*) Bad management etc.

Misconduct is a serious form of indiscipline against the management. According to the Gujarat High Court misconduct includes:

(*i*) Where the act of worker is inconsistent with the peaceful discharge of his duty towards his employee.

(*ii*) Where act of the employee make it unsafe for the employer to retain him in service.

(*iii*) Where the act of employee is so grossly immoral that all responsible men should not trust that employee.

(*iv*) Where the conduct of employee is such as to open before him ways for not discharging his duties properly.

(*v*) Where the worker is abusive or he disturbs the peace at the place of his employment.

(*vi*) Where the employee is habitually negligent in respect of the duties for which is engaged.

According to the Bombay High Court the following acts contribute misconduct.

(*i*) Theft, fraud or dishonesty in connection with employer's business.

(*ii*) Illegal strike.

(*iii*) Breach of duty, absences without leave, non-performance of job, duties disobedience, of orders.

(*iv*) Breach of discipline, assaulting supervisor, disrupting relations with workers.

(*v*) Delinquencies like telling lies, disloyalty and corruption, damage to property and goodwill.

(*vi*) Disrespectful conduct, disrespectful outside conduct etc.

Measures to Reduce Indiscipline

It may be remembered that the labour is most important and organic or living factor of production because the people and the efficiency of the organization make the organizations ultimately depends upon the motivation and efficiency of the people working in the organization. A tactful human relations approach enables the management not only to keep labour force motivated but also to stimulate them to improve their performance to contribute towards the organizational goals. Hence it is obligatory on the part of management to avoid in disciplinary tendencies in the organization and if it arises then study and analyze the causes of indiscipline, to take necessary and effective measures.

It has been observed that in general non-fulfilment of the needs of the workers on account of lower upper wages tends to be the main cause of indiscipline. Hence a worker should be paid fair and reasonable wages to enable him to maintain himself and his family in good health by way of satisfying socio-economic needs of his family.

When the worker joins the organization he under the contact of employment agreed to do his work honestly and to be loyal to the organization. In return he expects suitable economic reward, security of employment, fair treatment, better working condition, prospects for promotion etc. hence in order to encourage him to devote himself to his job it is necessary to give freedom of expression of his feeling. And sentiments and to provide him amenities along with human relations approach is much useful.

The trade union leadership should be developed from within the labour force so that he can present the demands properly to the management. Various human resources management policies should be made more realistic, dynamic and progressive.

Disciplinary Action

Indiscipline is the result of several interacting factors like economic, social, and political cultural, psychological etc; it needs to be carefully handled.

(*a*) The principle of natural justice should be strictly applied while conducting enquiries and taking action. It includes:

- (*i*) The worker should be given an opportunity to present witnesses of his own choice on whom he relies.
- (*ii*) The worker should be given the right to cross-examine management's evidence.
- (*iii*) The evidence management should be taken in workers presence.
- (*iv*) No material should be used against the workers without giving him an opportunity to explain.
- (*v*) The enquiry against the worker should be fair and conducted by an impartial person.
- (*vi*) The punishment awarded should not be out of proportion to the misconduct committed.
- (*vii*) The management should act in good faith.
- (*viii*) A sence of fairness, reasonableness and fair opportunity must prevail.
- (*ix*) No punishment should be meted out unless all the steps laid down in the Domestic Enquiry Procedure are propely and completely carried out. Thus the two basic principles of natural justice be applied these are: (1) No man shall be judge of in his own cause and (2) Hear the other side.

(*b*) The principles of impartiality or consistency be adopted as implies that under identical situations there should be no marked difference in the action taken.

(*c*) The principle of impersonality or consistency be followed which means that the disciplinary authority should not have a sense of triumph when a delinquent employee is to be subjected to enquiry.

(*d*) The disciplinary authority should attend reasonable opportunity to the offender to defend him. The model standing orders state that "before dismissing an employee he should be given an opportunity to explain the circumstances alleged against him".

Procedure of Disciplinary Action

Under model standing orders the following procedure has to be followed before passing an order for suspension, dismissal or discharge.

(1) Preliminary Investigation

The first step of the procedure is to held a preliminary investigation with a view to finding out whether prima-facie case of is conduct exists or not.

(2) Issue of a Charge-sheet

On the basis of the prima facie case of misconduct being established, the management may proceed to issue a charge sheet to the concerned worker. The charge sheet does not imply punishment but it is notice of a charge that the worker is responsible for some misconduct and that the management wants to know about what the concerned worker has to say about it. Thus it provides an opportunity to the worker to explain about his conduct. Hence a charge sheet is also known as a "show cause notice". While framing the charge sheet it may be noted that:

(*i*) Each charge should be stated in very clear terms, it should be precise and not vague.

(*ii*) There should be separate charge for each allegation.

(*iii*) There should not be multiple charges for the same allegation.

(*iv*) Charges should not be related to any matter, which has been already decided. Thus a charge-sheet should be framed in writing, based upon a written complaint by same one. It should give details of allegation of offence or misconduct. It should indicate time within which the reply to the charge-sheet is submitted to the authorities. It requires the authorities to show cause why disciplinary action should not be taken against him. The charge-sheet may include the proposed penalty that will be imposed if the charges are found real and substantial in nature.

(3) Receiving Defendants Explanation

The worker has to submit his explanation within a reasonable time or he may request for extension for its submission. While preparing his case he should be allowed access to the documents which he considers necessary and provide necessary information required by him. If the reply is satisfactory the management may withdraw the charges immediately. But if the explanation is not satisfactory the inquiry will proceed.

(4) Suspension Pending Enquiry if Needed

In case of a grave misconduct and if it is in the interest of discipline and security of the organization, the management may suspend a worker even before the charge sheet is issued or an order of suspension may be given along with the charge-sheet under Section 10A of the Indian Employment (Standing Orders) Act, 1946 the suspensed worker is to be paid a susbsistence allowance equal to one half of his wages for first ninety days of suspension and three fourths of the wages for the remaining period of suspension if the delay in completion of proceedings against his is not due to his conduct.

(5) Notice of Enquiry

When the reply to the charge-sheet is received, three possibilities arise:

(*a*) The worker may admit the charge but the charge involves minor penalty. Then and award punishment.

(*b*) The worker may not admit the charge but the charge involves minor penalty. Then also the employer may proceed and award punishment without holding further enquiry.

(*c*) The worker may not admit the charge but the charge merits the major penalty. Then the employer has to hold the inquiry to investigate into charges against the worker. This inquiry is called as "Domestic enquiry".

When it is decided to conduct an Enquiry Officer, well versed in law or an outside expert will be appointed. Then the notice of enquiry has to be issued to the worker will in advance, indicating date time and place of enquiry along with the name of the enquiry officer so that the worker can prepare his case. He should keep all the relevant documents ready and bring witness also with him.

(6) Conducting Enquiry

On the appointed date and time the enquiry is to be conducted by the enquiry officer in the presence of the worker. It is necessary to explain to the worker about the process of enquiry, contents of charge-sheet and explanation about the procedure of enquiry. If he pleads innocent then enquiry has to be proceeded with. If an employee requests for another coworker to represent and assist him in the conducting his defense, the enquiry officer should allow him to do so.

If the worker does not turn up for the enquiry without notice or reasonable cause of refuses to participate or walks out then the enquiry officer may proceed to hold the enquiry 'ex-parte'. The person who provides evidence from the management side is called the presentation officer.

The details of the enquiry are to be recorded and signed by all the persons. Once all the witness against him are examined, the defense witness along with the worker have to submit their statements. All the relevant information documents and evidence may be examined in order to arrive at certain conclusion.

(7) Recording of the Findings by the Enquiry Officer

When the process of the enquiry is completed the enquiry officer has to give his findings along with the procedure of enquiry, the parties heard the documents examined, the charges made and the explanation given the evidence produced and finally his findings about each charge separately. Then he has to submit his findings to the authority in charge of disciplinary action. However he is not required to make any recommendation, it is to be decided by the appropriate authority.

(8) Decision of the Disciplinary Authority

If the authority accepts the findings, then he has to decide; but if he rejects the findings he may order a fresh enquiry or let matter drop. While deciding he will take into consideration the evidence and decide about penalty, keeping in mind the previous record of service of the offender. When the decision is arrived at, its has to be in writing.

(9) Communication of the Order of Punishment

The employee is given the final order in writing along with clear statement of the charges establishment, the punishement awarded and the reason thereof and the date from which punishment is to be effective. When the order of the punishment is served the domestic enquiry is concluded.

It should be noted that all the documents should carefully preserved for future reference because the standing orders provide for appeals against any order by which the worker is aggrieved.

In case of dispute which is pending in conciliation, arbitration or adjudication proceedings the employer has no right to punish workman for his misconduct that is connected with pending dispute.

Objectives and Functions

The origin of wage boards can be traced back to 1930's when the Royal Commission on Labour recommended the settings up of tripartite boards in Indian industries. However the British Government neglected it. After independence the First Five Year Plan stated that "permanent wage boards with a tripartite composition should be set up in each state and the centre, to deal comprehensively with all aspects of the questions of wages, to initiate necessary inquiries, collect data, review the situation from time to time and take decision regarding inquiries, collect data, review the situation from time to time and take decision regarding wage adjustments suo-moto or on reference from the parties or from Government. The Second Plan also insisted upon the need for determining wages through industrial wage boards. The recommendations of the Indian Labour Conference in 1957 and several other industrial committees, the Government had to take a decision to set up the First Wage Board in the cotton textile and sugar industries in 1957. It was also influenced by the report of ILO.

Generally the demand for settings of wage boards comes from union. In India, the Bomaby Industrial Relations (Amendment) Act of 1948 is the earliest legislation providing for the establishment of wage boards in any industry covered by Act. So it was set up for the cotton textile industry to relieve Industry courts and Labour courts of a part of their adjudication work.

Objectives of Wage Boards

According to the National Commission of Labour the objectives of the Boards are:

(*i*) To create a climate for harmonious industrial relations.

(*ii*) To safeguard the interest of the community and to represent consumers' interests.

(*iii*) To devise standardized wage structure for the concerned industry.

Functions of the Wage Board

The wage board function industry wise in broader framework which includes recommending:

(*i*) The minimum wage

(*ii*) Differential cost of living compensation

(*iii*) Regional wage differentials

(*iv*) Gratuity

(*v*) Hours of work etc.

(*vi*) Wage boards have to determine which categories of employee are to be brought within the scope of wage fixation.

(*vii*) They also workout the wage structure based on the principles of fair wages as suggested by fair wages committee.

(*viii*) They suggest a system of payment by results.

(*ix*) The wage boards work out the principles that should govern bonus to workers in industries.

Thus the wage boards have to carry out a large number of important functions. However the fixation of wage seals on an industry basis has been considered as a challenging task before them.

Evaluation of the Performance of Wage Board

(*i*) According to K.N. Vaid the wage boards are of the ways of working out the principle of voluntary arbitration. But the experience of the working of boards shows that unions regard them as substitute for compulsory adjudication and an extension of the process of collective bargaining. This is the result of the attitude of the employers who do not take interest in implementing decisions of wage boards.

(*ii*) The main purpose of wage boards was to calculate and fix fair wages, but the study of their functioning reveals that they aremore concened with fixing wages that would cover the established norms rather than the fair wage that is related to capacity of industry to pay while doing so they have duplicated the function prescribed the minimum wages committees.

(*iii*) The wage boards are functioning as a negotiating machinery to adjust the differences of opinion between employers and their labour in arriving at an acceptable mean.

(*iv*) The wage boards made a big change by way of merging the dearness allowance with the basic wage, which is seen in case of textile industry. They divided country into regions accordingly to dearness or cheapness of the locality and allowance granted on varying basis.

(*v*) While fixing fair wages the wage boards have followed thenorms stated by the committees on fair wages and later on ratified at the 15th session of the Indian Labour Conferece. There has been a lot of confusion in the application of the norms. The wage boards have not solved the problem of this confusion.

(*vi*) The boards are relatively successful in promoting industry wise negotiations and active participation by the parties in the determination of wages and other conditions of employment.

(*vii*) The national Commission on Labour identified that –

(*a*) A majority of the recommendations of wage boards are not unanimous.

(*b*) The time taken by the wage boards to complete their task has been very long.

(*c*) The implementations of the recommendations of the wage boards has been difficult.

(*viii*) However the commission concluded "The system of wage boards has on the whole, served useful purpose, as bipartite collective bargaining on wages and allied issues on industry wise basis at the national level has not been found practicable at present for various reasons, this system has provided the machinery for the same. It is true that the system has not only fully met all the expectations and particularly in recent years, there has been an erosion of faith in this system on the part of both, employers and employees. The committee convinced that these defects are not such as cannot be remedied".

Measures for Improving the Performance of the Wage Boards

The committee has made the following recommendations for improving the performance of the wage boards as follows:

(*i*) The chairman of wage board should be selected by the common consent of the organization of employee and employers in the industry concerned.

(*ii*) The future the wage should function essentially as machinery for collective marketing and should strive for unity.

(*iii*) Technical assessors and experts should assist the wage boards.

(*iv*) The terms of referene of wage boards should be decided by the government in consultation with the organization of employer and workers concerned.

(*v*) Central wage boards should be set up in the Union ministry of labour on a permanent basis to serve all wage boards through the supply of statistical and other material and lending of the necessary staff.

(*vi*) He unanimous recommendations of wage boards should be accepted and in case of lack of unanimity the government should hold the consultation with the organizations of employer and employee before taking a final decision.

(vii) The wage boards should not be set up under any statutes but their recommendations, as finally accepted by the government, should be made statutory binding on party.

(viii) For the industries covered by wage boards a permanent machinery should be created for follow up action.

(ix) The wage boards should complete their work in one year's time and the operation of its recommendation should be between two or three years after which the need for a subsequent wage board could be considered on merit.

Thus it may be concluded that the institutions of wage boards has become popular in India. The boards have been successful in promoting industry wise negotiations, encouraged greater participation by the parties, freedom in decision-making and their recommendations have been useful for improving efficiency in industry. However delays involved in working of the boards and imperfect implementation of its recommendations need to be attended urgently to make boards more effective and efficient.

(A) Joint Councils

(*i*) At every division on zonal level in any organization employing 100 or more employees shall have a joint council only those persons who are in the employment of the organization can be the member of council. The tenure of the council shall be of two years.

(*ii*) The chief executive of organization or of its division or zonal branch shall be the chairman of the joint council.

(*iii*) The joint council shall appoint one of its members as its secretary who will prepare the agenda record the minutes of meetings and report on implementation of the decision taken at every meetings. The management shall provide all facilities within the premises of organization.

(*iv*) The joint council shall meet wherever necessary but at least once in a quarter.

(*v*) Every decision of the council shall be on the basis of consensus and not by the process of voting. It shall be binding on both workers and management and shall be implemented within one month.

Functions

The main functions of the joint council are:

(*i*) The settlement of matters unsettled by unit level councils and arranging joint meetings for resolving inter council problems.

(*ii*) Review of working of the unit level council for improvement in the customer service and evolving best way of handling of goods traffic accounts etc.

(*iii*) Optimum production efficiency and fixation of productivity norms of man and machines for the unit as a whole.

(*iv*) Development skills of workers and adequate facilities for training.

(*v*) Awarding rewards for valuable and creative suggestions given by the workers.

(*vi*) Preparations of schedules of working laws and holidays.

(*vii*) General health welfare and safety measures for unit of the plant.

(*viii*) Optimum use of resources and producing quality products.

(B) Unit Councils

A new scheme of worker's participation in management in service and commercial organizations in public sector was announced in January 1977.

The scheme aimed at setting of unit councils in units employing 100 or more persons. The organization covered included hotels, restaurants, hospitals, railway and road transport, posts docks, schools, research institutions etc. the unit level councils are to eliminate factors which retard operation and improve methods of operation. The main functions of the councils include:

(*i*) To create conditions for achieving maximum efficiency.

(*ii*) Better customer services.

(*iii*) Higher productivity.

(*iv*) Climination of corruption and pilferage.

(*v*) Developing reward system which show ability in their areas.

(*vi*) The councils will be formed consisting of the equal number of representatives of the workers and management at each unit employing 100 or more workers to discuss day to day problems and find solutions.

(*vii*) If necessary a composite councils may be formed to served more than one unit.

(*viii*) Management in consultation with registered or recognized union may decide the number of unit councils and the departments to be attached to each council of the organization.

(*ix*) All the decisions of the unit councils shall be on the basis of consensus and not by voting.

(*x*) Every decision of the council shall be implemented by the parties concerned within a month.

(*xi*) Management shall make a suitable agreement for recording and maintenance of minutes of the meetings and appoint one of its representative as secretary for this purpose.

(*xii*) The council shall meet as frequently as necessary but at least once in a month.

(*xiii*) The chairman of the council shall be nominee of the management and vice chairman be elected from workers representatives in the council.

(C) Plant Councils

The plant council is formed as recommended by the study group on labour in September 1985. The scheme is applicable to all public sector units excepts those exempted by the government.

Features of the scheme:

(*i*) There shall be one plant council for the whole unit.

(*ii*) Each council shall consist 6 to 18 members. The representatives of workers and employees will be equal in number. One third of representatives of workers should come from supervisor's class.

(*iii*) Only such person actually employed in the organizational unit can be members of plant council.

(*iv*) Its tenure shall be for a period of three years.

(*v*) The chief executive of the unit shall be the chairman of the plant council while vice chairman shall be from the employees.

(*vi*) The council shall appoint one of its members as secretary and management shall provide necessary facilities to him in the premises.

(*vii*) The council shall meet at least once in a quarter.

(*viii*) Every decision of the council shall be on the basis of consensus and both by voting.

(*ix*) The decision so arrived at shall be implemented within a month.

(*x*) All unsettled issues shall be placed before Board of directors for their decision.

Functions of the Council

The Plant Council has to deal with a large number of functions which cover operational, economic, financial, personnel welfare environmental areas. It deals with:

(*i*) Determination of productivity schemes taken into consideration the local conditions.

(*ii*) Planning implementation, attainment and review of monthly targets and schedules.

(*iii*) Material supply and preventing its shortages.

(*iv*) Housekeeping activities.

(*v*) Improvement in productivity especially in critical areas.

(*vi*) Quality and technological improvements.

(*vii*) Machine utilization and development of new products etc.

(*viii*) Balance sheet profit and loss statements.

(*ix*) Review of operating expenses, financial results, cost of sales etc.

(*x*) Matters relating to absenteeism.

(*xi*) Problems of women workers.

(*xii*) Initiation and administration of workers programmes.

(*xiii*) Implementation of welfare schemes, such as medical facilities having transport facilities, safety measures etc.

(*xiv*) Control of habits of gambling, drinking and indebtedness etc. amongst workers.

(*xv*) Environmental protection.

(*xvi*) Extension activities and community development programmes.

(D) Shop Councils

The main features of shop council are as follows:

(*i*) In every unit employing 500 or more employees, the employer shall constitute a shop council for each shop or department or one council for several shops on the basis of number of employees employed in each department.

(*ii*) Each council shall consist of equal number of representatives of employers and employees.

(*iii*) Employees representatives must be from those who are actually working in the organization.

(*iv*) The number of members of each council may be determined by the employer in consultation with recognized union but the total number should be maximum 12.

(*v*) All the decisions of shop council shall be on the basis of consensus and not by the voting.

(*vi*) Every decision of shop council shall be implemented by parties concerned within the period of one month.

(*vii*) The shop council once formed shall function for three years.

(*viii*) The shop council shall meet as frequently as required but at least once in a month.

(*ix*) The chairman of the shop council shall be a nominee of management which voice chairman shall be the representatives of the employees.

Functions of Shop Council

The shop council are responsible for increasing production productivity, economy and deficiency of the organization. It has to look after the following:

1. To identify the areas of low productivity and take necessary steps to improve the performance.
2. To study the absenteeism and recommend steps to reduce it.
3. To assist in maintaining general discipline in the organization.
4. To review welfare facilities and suggest improvements in them.
5. To study working conditions and suggest measures to improve them.
6. To maintain two ways flow of communication between workers and management especially in case of production schedule and progress towards achieving targets.
7. To suggest technological innovations.
8. Quality improvement programmes.
9. To develop and implement work system design.
10. To assist in implementation of cost reduction techniques.
11. To formulate plans for multiple skill development programmes.
12. To supervise group working system.
13. To take periodic review of utilization of machinery and equipment.

The scheme is claimed to be successful in several public sector undertakings.

Role of Personnel and Industrial Relations Manager in Promoting Industrial Relations

These are as follows:

1. To create and utilize an able and motivated workforce, to accomplish the basic organizational goals.

2. To establish and maintain sound organizational structure and desirable working relationships among all the members of the organization.
3. To secure the integration of individual and groups within the organization by coordination of the individual and group goals with those of the organization.
4. To create facilities and opportunities for individual or group development so as to match it with the growth of the organization.
5. To attain an effective utilization of human resources in the achievement of organizational goals.
6. To identify and satisfy individual and group needs by providing adequate and equitable wages, incentives, employee benefits and social security and measures for challenging work, prestige, recognition, security, status etc.
7. To maintain high employee morale and sound human relations by sustaining and improving the various conditions and facilities.
8. To strengthen and appreciate the human assets continuously by providing training and developmental programmes.
9. To consider and contribute to the minimization of socio-economic evils such as unemployment, under-employment, inequalities in the distribution of income and wealth and to improve the welfare of the society by providing employment opportunities to women and disadvantaged sections of the society etc.
10. To provide and opportunity for expression and voice in management.
11. To provide fair, acceptable and efficient leadership.
12. To provide facilities and conditions of work and creation of favourable atmosphere for maintaining stability of employment.

The Code of Discipline 1948

The Code of Discipline 1948: In spite of a large number of labour laws, key role played by Indian courts in rendering justice in industrial relations. It is observed that the industrial relations seen in India is not satisfactory. The relation between worker and management tend to under strain and the workers involvement has not made progress. The Second Five Year Plan stated, "while the observance of stricter discipline, both o the part of labour and management, is matter which cannot be imposed by legislation, it has to be achieved by organization of employees and workers by evolving suitable sanctions on their own".

The code of discipline was accepted by Four Central National Labour Organizations INTUC, AITUC, HMS, UTUC, on behalf of workers and by the employers federation of India, the All India Organization of Industrial Employers and All India Manufacturers Organization on behalf of the employers.

Objectives of the Code of Discipline

The Code has been aimed at the established healthy industrial relations between management and workers on voluntary basis to promote harmony and to get rid of industrial conflicts.

According to the Third Five Year Plan "The Code plays down specific obligations for the management and the worker with the object of promoting constructive co-operation between their representatives at all levels, avoiding stoppages as well as litigation's, security settlement of grievances by mutual negotiations, conciliation and voluntary arbitration, facilitating the growth of trade union and eliminating all forms of coercion and violence in industrial relations".

Main Features of the Code

(*i*) The Code of Discipline in government induced, self imposed and mutually agreed voluntary principle of discipline and relations between management and workers in industry.

(*ii*) The code aims at preventing industrial disputes by providing for voluntary and mutual settlement of disputes through negotiation conciliation voluntary arbitration without interference of external agency or through adjudication.

(*iii*) It restrains both the parties from unilateral action but it induces them to make the best use of the existing machinery for the settlement of disputes with the almost expedition.

(*iv*) Strikes and lockouts cannot be declared without prior notice.

(*v*) The parties should not take any action without consulting each other.

The code does not have any legal sanction but the following moral sanctions are behind it.

(*a*) The central organizations of employees and workers shall take necessary step against their constituent units when they are guilty of breaches of the code.

(*b*) Grave, willful and persistent breaches of the code by any parts should be widely publicized.

(*c*) Failure to observe the code would entail de recognition, normally for the period of one year but it may be changed by concerned implementing committee.

(*d*) A dispute may not ordinarily be referred for adjudication if there is a strike or lockout without proper notice or in breach of the code on determined by the implementation machinery unless such strikes or lockout is called off.

Inter Union Code of Conduct 1958

It was voluntarily adopted by the four central organizations of the labour INTUC, AITUC, HMS, UTUC, in May 1958.

The main objective of the Code was "To reduce inter-union rivalry, to achieve trade union amity and to remove the ills which had developed in the labour management relations and in the labour movements".

The four central organizations of the worker agreed on the following issues for the purpose of maintaining harmonious inter union relations. The Code states:

(*i*) Every employee in an industry or unit shall have the freedom and right to join union of his choice. No coercion shall be exercised in this matter.

(*ii*) There shall be no dual membership of unions.

(*iii*) There shall be unreserved acceptance of and respect for the democratic functioning of trade unions.

(*iv*) There shall be regular and domestic elections of executive bodies and office-bearers of trade unions.

(*v*) Ignorance and backwardeness of workers shall not be exploited by any organization, no organization shall make excessive or extravagant demands.

(*vi*) All unions shall eschew casteism communalism and provincialism.

(*vii*) There shall be no violence, coercion intimidation or personal vilification in inter union dealings.

(*viii*) All central organizations shall assist in the formation on continuance of company union.

The code was based on voluntary spirit rather than legal compulsion. It aimed at avoiding inter-union rivalries. It had some impact on inter union relations. But mostly the code has been breached and every clause of the code has been quite often violated on a large scale by every union in India.

Industrial Truce Resolution 1962

The Chinese attack in October 1962 led to the declaration of Emergency in India. It was realized that the productive activities in the country should not suffer on any count. The joint meeting of employers and workers, representatives was held in November 1962 and it passed the resolution that "No effort shall be spared to achieve maximum production, and management and workers will have to collaborate in all possible ways to promote the defense efforts of the country".

It was also "re-affirmed that they would take the pledge of unstinted loyalty and devotion to the country and agreed to create favourable climate to promote constructive co-operation between management and workers and not to interrupt or slow down production work on extra shift and extra hours and make efforts to ensure price stability".

As a result of this resolution, there was significant decline in the number of industrial disputes as well as the man-days lost. The workers not only hard for extra hours but also contributed to the National Defense Fund substantially.

The resolution emphasized on the following aspects:

(*i*) To create suitable climate and preserve it for ensuring sustained efforts and actions to achieve the aims.

(*ii*) To maintain industrial peace and promote cordial relations between labour and management.

(*iii*) To maintain steady flow of production by way of avoiding all the events that cause interruption in the production process and to increase production by way of working overtime, even on Sundays if necessary.

(*iv*) To make efforts to maintain price stability in case of industrial goods and essential commodities.

(*v*) To increase savings in the larger interest of the nation both by worker and

(*vi*) Management and workers be persuaded to contribute liberally to the Nations Defence Fund. Emergency Production Committees were set up at the centre and in the states to improve production and productivity.

However, the resolution lost its importance as prices started rising rapidly and disputes started erupting again.

Grievance Handling

With whatever the attitudes and good intentions with which a company works and manages it workmen, some dissatisfaction is created, for it is difficult to satisfy every person in every aspect in the company. Thus there is hardly any company where its employees have no grievance against the company. These grievances may be real or imaginary. Most often these are resulting out of some misunderstanding or wrong interpretation of some rule, policy or action taken by management.

Grievance produces unhappiness over the environment, indifference to the sincerity towards the company, and results in low morale at work. Organisation is the greater looser in the process. Grievance is corrosion on industrial relations. It all depends upon its handling by the staff and officers in the company. The first person plays a very significant role in such a situation, for he is the one who knows a real cause and how it was misled, or quoted wrongly. Drawing instant closure to such a grievance is a must, for the cost of a stretched grievance could be very high in terms of poor work performance, poor efficiency and damaging the whole atmosphere in the company.

While directing efforts towards better processing of employee complaints, a well designed, defined and well monitored procedure for handling grievances, goes a long way in ensuring better industrial relations. Effective grievance administration not only helps in reduction of complaints but elimination of many to certain extent over a period of time. The system therefore should include and stress upon the areas like better communications skills and channels in use, redesigning of job descriptions and titles, so that minor complaints can be removed in the first place. Moreover the shop and office atmosphere should be free and open for any one to speak out and express his or her opinion on the given task or work situation. Complaints regarding work come to the surface only in such environment.

Definition

Grievance has been defined in different words. According to Prof. Jucius it is, "any discontent or dissatisfaction, whether expressed or not, whether valid or not, arising out of anything connected with the company that an employee thinks, believes or even feels is unfair, unjust or inequitable". According to Keith Davis it is, "any real or imagined feeling of personal injustice which an employee has concerning his employment relationship".

It is observed that three terms – dissatisfaction, complaint and grievance – indicate various forms and stages of employee dissatisfaction. These all forms means it is the feeling of anything that disturbs an employee whether he expresses or not. Grievance is a simple complaint, spoken or written, that has been ignored, overridden, or dismissed without due consideration. This dismissal could be by any shop supervisor or by an officer or a manager while handling any of his subordinates.

Grievance is a complaint by one or more workmen covering areas related to wages, allowances, conditions of work, overtime working, leave, transfer, promotion, seniority, job assignment termination of services etc. As regards the broader classification of these is concerned, these many fall under categories like discipline matters, supervisor behaviour, working conditions and rules, violation of terms of contract etc.

Practice of Handling Grievances

The National Commission on Labour also has defined a grievance as "complaints affecting one or more individual workmen in respect of their wage payments, overtime, leave, transfer, promotion, seniority, work assignment and discharges would constitute grievance". The method of presenting a grievance could be formal or informal, it could be in oral or in written format. Recent practice in grievance handling has been towards a formal procedures. Formal procedural matters get more serious attention than the informal matters and complaints.

Most enterprises have a formal system of grievance handling wherein a written complaint is sought to attract attention from the seniors. This is normally as per the pattern followed by Indian Labour Conference while presenting its model. The employee needs to be free from any restraint or coercion, because an aggrieved workman is likely to be more emotionally upset and thus he shall not be in a position to put forth his problems to his superiors, in a more systematic pattern.

However, first reporting of any grievance to the first line supervisor and its immediate settlement at that level is very important, since most of the grievances originate at the shop floor level. It is our experience that first line officers and managers are more familiar with the problems related and originated at the shop floor level and thus they are proved to be more capable to handle those. The success of the settlement process lies in the skill, fairness, understanding and good judgement used by the concerned person. It is also found that the first level supervisors or foremen or managers are side lined, due to increasing influence of unions on the shop floor, while handling minor disputes.

Sometimes the officers themselves shirk the responsibility and pass on the matters to personnel department, as the specialist department. A system for a long-term solution is necessary to strengthen these first line officers through continuous exposures and training and guidance on personal counselling, involvement in cases, delegation from the seniors, feedback and review of previous cases, or even through real life case study sessions. Grievances from shop are really interesting and managers can learn the values of persuasion, and hard realities of gaining co-operation from a group which is heterogenous in nature.

A manager trained on shop, specially a technocrat knowing his job fully well, gets a clear acceptance from the workmen, for they believe in him more as regards his capacity to understand better the shop situations and problems. Since his main objective is to get the job done in a stipulated time schedule, his approach is always to settle, compromise and sort out the matter than to argue as to who is right or who is wrong. This is the difference between the approach of persons from other departments where they may give more importance to the rules and procedural part.

Role of Personnel Department

Grievance handling should not be the monopoly of a specialist or the functional department. Role of personnel department should be that of a co-ordinating agency in both, understanding the problem and assisting the functional department in resolving the issue. The personnel department should act in a very flexible manner, with a sole objective to handle any grievance in a decent maner without disturbing the feelings and role of any person or a department. The personnel department therefore should take the responsibility to :

1. Devise a sound grievance procedure with effective upward communication system.
2. Advise the on-line-people about the importance of a sound system and its implementation.
3. Arrange training of staff and on line officers on effective handling of grievance through better inter personal and counselling skills.
4. Implement promptly the decisions arrived after the grievance procedure is over.
5. Maintain effective and close liaison with all the persons concerned.
6. Maintain all records on proceedings of the grievances.

7. Follow up, take review, after having discussions with all the persons, of the procedure, and if necessary modify it according to the changes, with suggestions from others.
8. Maintain rapport with cases handled, so as to create an atmosphere of confidence amongst other employees in the organisation.

It is also duty of the personnel department to periodically evaluate the existing system of grievance handling through some exercises on rate of grievances, rate of settlements and the satisfaction levels achieved there. A senior person can also formulate a set of questions and get answers as a feedback on the overall procedure from persons even unconnected with.

Some Principles

Some important parameters of a sound grievance procedure are the maintenance of related data, its analysis and research which can help improve the performance of the total handling system. Such analysis provides insight into the group dynamics and informal relationships which are existing within the group and its leader. Similarly constant collection, analysis and interpretation of grievance data can provide the management with a very valuable feedback about a situation.

Grievances must be settled as near as possible to the point of origin and on merit only. Hasty actions, without collecting enough details and ascertaining facts, lead to further aggravation of the situation. Hence, it is better to have a simple, fair and easy to understand system, where by workmen easily get encouraged to put forth the facts and their complaints. This is the healthy sign of good relations between the employees and the officers which strengthens the bonds between them.

Enlightened management of the company should expect complaints and grievances. If a company officers state that, it does not have any grievances, for it could be a sign of suffering relationships, where people are afraid to speak out and seniors are left in dark, but may be caught napping on some other occasion! Therefore, ineffective mechanism to handle grievance can lead to increasing employee unrest. Therefore grievance procedure should be effectively used for identifying areas of conflicts in the union and management relationship and to resolve those for the overall benefits of the both the parties.

Index

T